## Contributors

Anita Gordeuk Backenstose

Sandra DeBella Baldigo

Barbara A. Bergeron

Claude T. Bergeron

Monica Jean Davis

Laura Deluca Douville

Elaine Elizabeth Dye-White

Frank T. Farnkopf

Arlene Parrish Gray

Jane Henneman

Katherine Jensen

Jeannie B. Maes

Virginia Young Meyer

Sylvia Novak

Diane Rowe

Phyllis Schubert

Sue Thomas

Wendy Votroubek

# PRECEPTORSHIPS
# IN
# NURSING EDUCATION

## Sandra Stuart-Siddall
## Jean M. Haberlin

Rural Clinical Nurse Placement Center
California State University at Chico

AN ASPEN PUBLICATION®
Aspen Systems Corporation
Rockville, Maryland
Royal Tunbridge Wells

1983

Library of Congress Cataloging in Publication Data

Main entry under title:

Preceptorships in nursing education.

Includes bibliographies.
1. Nursing—Study and teaching (Preceptorship)
2. Nursing—Study and teaching (Preceptorship)—
United States. I. Stuart-Siddall, Sandra.
II. Haberlin, Jean. [DNLM: 1. Education,
Nursing. 2. Preceptorship. WY 18.5 S932p]
RT74.7.P73 1983     610.73'07'1     83-2772
ISBN: 0-89443-936-7


Publisher: John Marozsan
Editorial Director: Darlene Como
Executive Managing Editor: Margot Raphael
Editorial Services: Scott Ballotin
Printing and Manufacturing: Debbie Collins

Library of Congress Catalog Card Number: 83-2772
ISBN: 0-89443-936-7


*Printed in the United States of America*

2  3  4  5

# Table of Contents

# Foreword

A preceptor can be viewed as an amalgam, pursuing the activities of a teacher or tutor and the work of a student involved in a technical operation or, as described by one of the chapter authors, following "a clearly defined course of study that will meet the individual's needs and match the students' interests while the attainment of identified professional goals is achieved."

Members of the nursing faculty are responsible for applying advances in all areas of technical, biological, and human sciences. They also are held accountable for providing opportunities that allow for individualized learning in an environment encouraging a high level of accomplishment. The student is responsible for actively participating in the learning process and assisting in designing experiences beneficial to reaching self-defined goals. This teaching-learning combination in nursing is undertaken with full recognition of the need to provide safe, effective, and ethical care to the patient.

The use of preceptors in the clinical nursing setting moves the student experience away from the traditional or stereotypical model of clinical instruction. *Preceptorships in Nursing Education* provides a comprehensive review of preceptorships by first discussing the use of clinical preceptors from the faculty's perspective, advantages of using preceptorships, locating and selecting preceptors, designing courses, utilizing and orienting preceptors, establishing rapport, and feeling comfortable while using preceptors.

The second part of the text provides insight into the role of a preceptor by discussing the needs and challenges of such a position. The third and fourth parts explain experiences, needs, and personal gains of the student. The administrator's point of view is presented in relation to legal considerations, criteria of evaluation, and the necessity of having a supportive administration. The final portion of the book is devoted to the responsibility shared by faculty members and preceptors in providing for change and innovation in nursing education programs.

The use of preceptors in nursing education has become increasingly important as student experience has moved beyond the walls of acute care facilities and into community agencies. Preceptors have been essential to nurse practitioner preparation and vital to registered nurse-baccalaureate in nursing programs. *Preceptorships in Nursing Education* should find a substantial audience of faculty members in schools of nursing and students enrolled in programs using the preceptorship model.

The authors of the various chapters throughout the text are well prepared to present the theoretical concepts, since they have had extensive experience in assisting students in this important area of independent learning. Their educational endeavors include experience in nurse practitioner programs, contractual learning with baccalaureate students, and placement of students in rural clinical sites. *Preceptorships in Nursing Education* is an important contribution to nursing educational literature.

*Mary Lou McAthie, R.N., Ed.D.*
Special Assistant/
Regional Nursing Program Consultant
Department of Health and Human Services

# Part I

# Using Clinical Preceptors To Teach Clinical Nursing— The Faculty Perspective

# Chapter 1

# Trends in Nursing Education

*Sandra Stuart-Siddall*

A great many changes have occurred in nursing and nursing education over the last ten years. Some of the changes have been painful; maybe all of them have been painful in some respect. But ultimately most of them have been beneficial. And there are still more to come.

What is in store for nursing education? My optimistic response is that, given the merging of certain conditions, nursing education will be challenging and enlightening, will promote the science of nursing and not medicine, and will become more efficient.

Nursing educators and nursing service leaders are discussing curriculum content and identifying the level of skill they desire to see in graduating nurses. Nurse educators will be responsible for determining the way theory and skills will be taught; nursing service professionals will be responsible for ensuring that their facilities provide opportunities for students to gain the necessary skills and practice.

I think one good turn deserves another. If nursing service personnel want to help in curriculum design and course content, they should welcome the help of nursing educators in improving working conditions for nurses and in designing and implementing creative strategies to change the things that make staff nursing so difficult and frustrating for nurses today.

## PROBLEMS AND SOLUTIONS

Too often, groups of professional nurses are still blaming each other for the problems that produce nurse frustration and poor nurse preparation. As is typical of a profession undergoing change, we have spent years pointing fingers, repeatedly defining the problems, and spending countless frustrating hours meeting rather than taking concrete steps to effect plans to improve conditions for nurses. Now, I believe the time has finally come to implement these plans.

In talking to nursing administrators in hospitals and clinics around the country, I have become aware of the many efforts being made to improve nursing in these facilities and to bring satisfaction and real rewards to nurses—real, tangible, measurable rewards, not merely token rewards. I have spent hours on the telephone, talking to directors of nursing in hospitals in Maine, Georgia, Texas, Utah, Arizona, and Michigan to find out what they are doing to make life better for the professional nurses in their facilities. Of course they cannot create change singlehandedly. The lack of money and other obstacles encountered by hospital administrators and their communities and medical staffs pose formidable roadblocks. Still, most hospitals are, in fact, doing something. For example, incentives are being identified to help nurses stay in nursing. Job descriptions are being modified so that levels, and expectations of those levels, are helping nurses to determine what they have to do and where they have to go, horizontally and vertically, to be promoted upward in the facility. Systems for getting more input and feedback from staff nurses are being developed in some hospitals. Though unquestionably nurses are not earning anywhere near what they deserve, most hospitals are trying to provide higher salaries. More or different benefits are being identified; choices in shifts and the hours the shifts cover are being offered; and different types of nursing care and nursing approaches (team or primary care) are being tried. Finally, benefits are being individualized or personalized: shifts, hours worked, and the specialties of nursing are all being reexamined as hospitals try to put the jigsaw puzzle together.

## OUR CHANGING NURSING SCHOOLS

Nursing schools are also undergoing great change. Nursing faculties are aware that changes are needed. While legislators are concerned about dollars, nursing service personnel are concerned about staffing, and state board or National League for Nursing (NLN) representatives are concerned with quality education and are pressuring nursing educators and institutions of nursing education to change accordingly.

Despite pressures and attacks from all sides, nurse educators are rising to the challenge. They are altering approaches to teaching; they are questioning and changing the units required for a degree or the major; they are redesigning curricula; and they are constructing simulation labs, utilizing more mediated teaching packets, testing more closely the skill levels of prospective graduates, and assessing more carefully the levels of confidence and the professional attitude of the graduates.

One of the personally satisfying changes I see taking place is the growing awareness of the need to increase nursing science and research. This trend has been coupled with the long-overdue effort to get away from teaching by the medical model, the method that has been traditionally adhered to in the teaching of nursing.

The shift of some faculty members away from being all things to their students—the role model, the lecturer, the mother surrogate, the disciplinarian, the "sage," the friend or social comrade, the clinical expert—is also refreshing. No one can be all these things to students in a discipline and at the same time expect cognitive or affective growth from them.

Traditional approaches and roles are hard to alter. But these changes in nursing education and service are necessary. Change means letting go of the old, comfortable ways that were becoming destructive to the profession. Yet, though some of the changes nurse educators are undergoing are disturbing and uncomfortable, others are painless and refreshing. As one might expect, attitude plays a significant role in how change is going to affect an individual. Responses may range from, "Who gives a damn!" to "Go with the flow," to "I've done it this way for 20 years," to "Great, we needed it!" Some faculty fear the unknown—new techniques, exposures to new people, even changes in their job descriptions. Some faculty get pulled out of ruts that were comfortable—patterns that may have been successful in the past but in which there is much room for improvement. Fear makes people retaliate and become defensive and uncooperative. Thus, inevitably, those who fear change will slow down a process that otherwise might take much less time, money, and personal trauma to accomplish.

One of the simpler improvements tried by some faculty has been to shift from hand-graded tests to computerized tests. Such a change requires the altering of test questions and test styles and, in some cases, the redesigning of the test. Although the intent is to save thousands of hours of faculty time in hand scoring, complaints about "relying on a computer to grade a test" and being forced to change the testing format were widespread.

Another simpler type of change was to involve entire faculty groups in curriculum design and updating. Instead of just the department head and one assistant being responsible for designing course and curriculum content and the program sequence toward the degree, the faculty meet together as a group to propose ways to help their programs comply with state and national academic and professional standards. The resulting merging of different philosophies and perspectives provides a new depth and richness to such efforts. There is, of course, at times a conflict of philosophies, but the final compromise is usually a better product than one can get from just one or two minds.

Formerly, faculty members dealt with course design and content without too much interference or peer review. Now, though course outlines are still the responsibility of the faculty teaching the course, several people are usually involved in monitoring the ultimate results. A team of faculty members is assigned the responsibility for a course subject, and several persons get together to plan and design the content.

This new check and balance system brings together the best of many backgrounds and experiences. Yet it too has met with much resistance— some well-founded and some ill-founded. Some responses are defensive: "Doesn't the school or chairperson trust me anymore?" or "I have been teaching this subject for 12 years; no one can show me a better way to teach it." The valid complaints usually focus on the problems one encounters in any group situation—personality conflicts, an emerging leader who is intimidating and unapproachable or unchallengeable, extreme philosophies of teaching approaches or grading procedures, and so on.

Assertiveness training over the last few years has been beneficial in resolving some aspects of this group-process problem. Sensitive and aware chairpersons try to designate team members who are compatible. It is a great mistake to think that everyone will enhance the esprit de corps in a program. Politics, cliques, and human errors cause many problems in the group process. Nonetheless, faculty who work together on curriculum design can more quickly spot weaknesses and gaps in the total course sequence of their nursing programs. It is only natural that individual faculty members will protect primarily their own specialty or subject. In some cases, they will feel that, as long as their turf is adequately covered, the rest is up to someone else. As a united group, however, they will also see where some subjects are being taught repetitiously and where other subjects are being totally ignored.

Another outcome of this collegial process is that the chairperson no longer has to bear alone the burden of enforcing state and national requirements. The chairperson can delegate the enforcement of these regulations to the faculty to make sure that the curriculum reflects the necessary standards.

Finally, in this joint process, a faculty member who wants to overemphasize a favorite specialty subject in the curriculum may no longer be able to do so. For example, a faculty member who feels that at least 20 units of med-surg should be taught, following the precedent of many years, would be confronted by a new structure of faculty involvement and meetings that would temper the member's zeal for med-surg and produce some sort of compromise.

Here is another example of such a compromise: At one college where I taught, a small group of tenured faculty had for years been "calling the shots" for the entire faculty. This group emphasized the medical model and med-surg nursing. Over time, with newer faculty coming on board, it became evident that this overemphasis on med-surg and certain other subjects had made the curriculum less effective than it could be. But since no one wanted a protracted battle between the tenured, older conservatives and the newer faculty, a compromise on a new curriculum was reached. Everybody felt that communication, culture, spiritual needs, and social needs should remain as important parts of the curriculum. But everyone had something different to offer in these areas—different experiences, different approaches and different philosophies. It was clearly not acceptable that only one or two people should present their personal views on these subjects in just one semester. However, it so happened that the curriculum training in these subjects was in fact given solely in the first semester of nursing, along with many other basic physical nursing skills. Not wanting to give up this crucial portion of the first semester, the first semester faculty began to coalesce in opposition to the rest of the faculty.

In the meantime, the med-surg faculty were upset because beginning levels of med-surg nursing were being postponed in the nursing sequence of courses, often until the students reached third or fourth semester. The conflict escalated, with hard feelings growing among faculty members. Conservatives disputed with liberals concerning their favorite subjects and the amount of time or units spent in teaching them.

The solution? It was decided to establish the core concept. In each semester, the nursing communication skills and the social, religious, and cultural assessment skills were stratified so that all faculty members could deal with them in their own semesters. Med-surg was begun early in the first semester, because the stratification of the other subjects into other semesters left time for med-surg instruction to begin at that earlier point.

"Change for change's sake?" If I had a dime for every time I have heard someone complain that the only reason for such restructuring is merely to change something, I would be rich. More appropriately—and much easier on everyone's temperament—the judgment should be, "change for improvement's sake."

A more difficult change for faculty is to become better clinical role models or, in other words, to become more clinically competent. Over the past ten years, students have become more verbal, more visible, more involved; and they now have more to say about faculty performance. Many nursing faculty members have let their clinical skills deteriorate while they emphasized the preparation of lectures, the designing of tests, clinical assignments, and so on. Indeed, some nurse educators have never functioned clinically as nurses, even though they are well-prepared academically. Eventually, for a variety of reasons, including inadequacy as an instructor, this problem has become more visible. Of course, nursing is not the only discipline faced with this problem; faculty from other majors with clinical components also often lack actual clinical experience.

Some solutions are available to deal with this problem. Dual appointments have been implemented at some institutions. For example, the nursing faculty may teach nine months out of the year and, in the following three months, work in a nearby facility in the faculty members' own areas of teaching expertise. Another solution is for some of the faculty to go back to school during nonacademic periods to gain clinical certificates in specialty areas. Clearly, none of these is the perfect solution. But in these and other ways, it is possible for those faculty who teach a discipline where clinical contact is made to become current and skilled in the subject.

The list of such developing changes in nursing education is almost endless. The list ranges from personal and attitudinal changes to professional changes that encompass a variety of new and challenging teaching responsibilities and new and more efficient teaching approaches.

## THE PRECEPTOR ROLE

Of all the evolving changes in nursing education, the development of the preceptor role is certainly the most challenging and satisfying. As a clinical expert, role model, or supervisor, the preceptor has given new momentum to the student nurse's progression through a program. It is hard to imagine a better way to achieve a student nurse's behavioral objectives than by coupling the behavioral model with a preceptor assignment. As with all the changes we have cited, this educational model is still viewed by a minority of educators as too nontraditional and threatening. Yet, if one thinks about it carefully, this view is mistaken. From the onset of baccalaureate education, nursing students proceed without their instructors, on their own initiative, in order to meet course requirements in the clinical field, one on one, with public health nurses. Indeed, with 10 students, or in some cases 15 students, per instructor, staff nurses have often served informally as preceptors while the harried instructor tries to make the rounds with all of the students. The idea of being responsible for 10 to 15 students gives some faculty people the impression that they in fact are singlehandedly teaching their students nursing skills. How far from the truth! In fact, nursing educators have utilized preceptors for years. Only now the concept is becoming formalized.

In subsequent chapters, we present the advantages of using preceptors formally in our profession. As nurse educators, we must be grateful to the thousands of clinical experts that, in this way, are helping us teach our students to be competent and confident clinical nurses.

# Chapter 2

# The Use of Clinical Preceptors

*Anita Gordeuk Backenstose*

The use of clinical preceptors, considered an instructional innovation by many nurse educators, is in fact not new. In the fields of medicine, dentistry, veterinary medicine, pharmacology, architecture, osteopathic medicine, and the ministry the most competent practitioners have long been used as mentors or preceptors to teach students via their own practices (Christman, 1979; Mauksch, 1980). In this chapter, we will discuss the historical and present use of clinical preceptors and examine the advantages of and the criteria for selecting them.

## HISTORICAL USE OF CLINICAL PRECEPTORS

The nursing literature regarding the clinical preceptor concept, though sparse, reflects the belief that preceptorships are a new approach to clinical instruction for many nursing programs (Adams, 1980; Chickerella & Lutz, 1981; Crancer, Fournier, & Maury-Hess, 1975; Ferguson & Hauf, 1973; Hall, 1977; Mahr, 1979; Walters, 1981; Wilson, Vaughan, & Gaff, 1977). Historically, however, the use of clinical preceptors is not a new concept in nursing.

Initially, nursing students were taught by practicing nurses. Nursing education and nursing service were closely tied; nursing service directors were also directors of nursing education, and nursing faculty were part of the hospital nursing staff. As nursing education moved to the academic setting in pursuit of professional growth, the service-education bond began to break. Faculty were physically removed from the practice setting and education-service interaction decreased. Faculty positions required a higher level of education than positions in nursing service, which further widened the gulf. Nursing students came to be taught didactically and clinically by nonpracticing nurse educators. As the nursing profession matured, the nursing service began to realize that broader and more specialized education would enhance nursing care, and staff nurses were encouraged to seek additional education at the baccalaureate and master's levels, thus bringing nursing education and service a bit closer together.

The clinical preceptor concept was reintroduced to nursing education with nurse practitioner programs in the 1960s (Mahr, 1979; Taylor, 1975). Nurse practitioner programs were designed to use clinical preceptors formally to meet specific educational objectives. Physicians were first used as preceptors, since nurses lacked the skills and experience to teach by asking for complete histories, performing physical examinations, or assessing and managing certain health problems (Taylor, 1975). Thus, the use of clinical preceptors was not new to the medical profession. Indeed, the effectiveness of preceptorships as a teaching method has been well documented in medical literature (Friedman, Baker, & Paige, 1979; Harris & Blum, 1977; Stritter, Hain, & Grimes, 1975). (Although a controversy exists among nurse educators regarding the use of medical preceptors for nursing students, that discussion is beyond the scope of this chapter.)

Since the 1960s, clinical preceptors have gained credibility as effective teachers in the nursing profession. Clinical preceptors have been widely used in nurse practitioner programs to provide students with an advanced level of clinical competency and an opportunity for role socialization. Certain undergraduate nursing programs have also begun to use clinical preceptors. One program has used the preceptor concept in an effort to draw education and service closer together (Clark, 1981). Many undergraduate preceptorships are offered as elective courses in which students are given direct supervision by nurses employed by the clinical agency in a specialty area (Crancer et al., 1975; Mahr, 1979). Other programs have used preceptors during practica just prior to graduation to decrease reality shock (Chickerella & Lutz, 1981; Walters, 1981) or as a means of providing quality student learning when an increased number of students need selected experiences in a variety of settings with a limited number of faculty to supervise the experience (Adams, 1980; Ferguson & Hauf, 1973). We have used clinical preceptors for undergraduate students to enable a greater number of students to have primary care experiences in small, geographically dispersed, rural community agencies. Still other programs have used clinical preceptors to allow students to meet individual objectives (Wilson et al., 1977). Regardless of the reason for using a clinical preceptor, the preceptorship generally has been viewed as a positive, worthwhile experience by students, faculty, and the clinical preceptors themselves. The struggle nursing has had in its academic and clinical professional growth confirms the need for sound education of students in nursing theory and

e use of clinical preceptors is one way to integrate the
and practice.

## USING A CLINICAL PRECEPTOR

Educators in the health professions have noted that the use of clinical preceptors can benefit the student, the faculty, and the preceptor in various ways. Following is a discussion of the advantages of using a qualified clinical preceptor, based on our own experiences and the experiences of other faculty cited in the literature.

### Advantages for the Student

Students can derive valuable benefits from working with a qualified clinical preceptor. The use of clinical preceptors provides mechanisms for quality student learning when an educational program has a large number of students and a limited number of faculty. Important functions of clinical experiences in student learning are to attain role socialization and to gain competence and confidence in performing clinical skills. When using a qualified clinical preceptor, role socialization is enhanced since the student's role model is an active practitioner (Adams, 1980).

Specific benefits are derived from a practicing role model. One benefit is that preceptors, familiar with their own caseloads, are better prepared to choose appropriate patients for student learning (Hall, 1977). Hall noted that, due to familiarity with their clients, preceptors can assign students to care for clients with health problems that meet specific student learning interests or needs and can provide assistance to the student in managing the health problem with the clients' unique needs in mind. However, even though preceptors are more familiar with their clients, Hall found that both preceptor and student benefited and welcomed discussion of client assignments with faculty to make sure student and course objectives were being met.

In using clinical preceptors in a rural community health project, we noted that both graduate and undergraduate students gained a wealth of practical knowledge from their clinical preceptors. For example, students learned to provide effective health education with special regard to (1) the amount of information a client can assimilate in one session, (2) the simplicity of explanation and vocabulary needed when discussing health problems, and (3) the kinds of information needed by clients to maintain wellness and practice self-care. We also noted that qualified preceptors knew the current management theories regarding health care problems in their practices and that they discussed these management theories with the students. Students received "gems of wisdom" from their preceptors in becoming efficient, in adapting to problems with innovation and creativity, and in learning means to increase patient compliance.

As role models, clinical preceptors have demonstrated collaborative practices with other health professionals. Students in our own nursing program stated that their preceptorship provided more opportunity than any of their nonpreceptor clinical experiences to observe and experience collaboration with other disciplines, such as medicine and the social services, in providing health care to clients.

Faculty in some nursing programs have reported that student experience with a clinical preceptor has helped to ease the impact of reality shock (Adams, 1980; Chickerella & Lutz, 1981; Walters, 1981). These faculty found that exposure to an everyday practice of a clinical preceptor increased student awareness of frustrations experienced by nurses and allowed opportunity to discuss and work through conflicts within the setting. We ourselves have noted that preceptors also helped students to face reality by assisting them in placing priority on nursing activities, thus helping the students to gain a "feel for" where one can and cannot cut corners on busy days so that health care is not compromised.

Another major benefit students receive from having a clinical preceptor is the one-on-one learning relationship that allows close supervision and immediate feedback. Because of the individualized attention, preceptors are able to give professional nurture to students, and individual learning needs of students are better identified and met (Chickerella & Lutz, 1981; Crancer et al., 1975). Wilson et al. (1977) found the benefit of individualized attention to be especially important in their program of preparing registered nurses with considerable experience for a baccalaureate degree. Particularly in community health settings, students are able to experience colleagueship with their preceptors and assume more professional responsibility, which results in increased professional accountability.

It has also been noted that students benefit from a clinical preceptorship by gaining increased confidence and competence in performing clinical skills (Crancer et al., 1975; Mentink, Trolinger, & O'Hara-Devereaux, 1980). In studies done by medical educators, students with a clinical preceptor had more competence in performing clinical skills than did nonprecepted students (Harris & Blum, 1977). Some students benefited from a learning experience with a clinical preceptor by becoming employed at the agency where the experience was obtained (Mentink et al., 1980; Crancer et al., 1975).

Research done on nurse practitioner students has revealed that preceptorships have had positive effects on the role socialization of students.

Sultz, Zielezny, and Kinyon (1976) found that nurse practitioners who had preceptorship experiences were more likely to practice the role after graduation than those who did not have a preceptorship. Malkemes (1974) has suggested that preceptorships are important for nurse practitioner students not only for role socialization but also for learning how to teach others about the role. Malkemes believes that such students should have physician clinical preceptors to help the physicians better understand and gain confidence in the competence of the nurse practitioner role.

## Advantages for the Faculty

Faculty from various nursing programs have experienced benefits from using a qualified clinical preceptor. Adams (1980) noted that the use of a clinical preceptor gave faculty more time to focus on making sure that students meet all course objectives. Faculty also had more time to provide specific guidance for students in applying knowledge and theory to practice. For example, faculty were able to place more emphasis on assisting students with specific learning needs in physical assessment skills, nursing techniques, communication skills, basic class content, and application of the nursing process. Adams was able to give more specific guidance to students during weekly student conferences and periodic site visits. Adams also found that using a clinical preceptor gave faculty increased visibility within the community. The close collegial relationships that developed between faculty, clinical preceptor, and other agency staff heightened the professional credibility of the faculty in the community. Crancer et al. (1975) reported that faculty were more likely to learn how the health community perceived the nursing program, both its strengths and its weaknesses. This author and the Crancer team also found that, by becoming better known in the health community, the faculty made more community contacts that could be used as resources for personal learning and student learning.

In our own studies, as in those done by Mauksch (1980), it was found that use of clinical preceptors provided more time for faculty to pursue their own clinical practices. Clinical practice provides professional stimulation to faculty, pushes them out of academic "ruts," helps them keep teaching relevant to practice, and provides opportunities for them to do clinical research. We believe that the use of clinical preceptors can also allow faculty to increase the emphasis on meeting requirements of scholarship by taking courses, attending conferences, doing consultation work, doing academic research, and writing scholarly papers.

It is important to note, however, that faculty have experienced some problems when using clinical preceptors. A great deal of planning and coordination is needed for a successful preceptorship, especially during the orientation phase. Faculty schedules must be flexible enough to help students with special learning needs and to give needed direction and feedback to preceptors and travel to various agencies when special problems arise. Adams (1980) points out that faculty have less contact with students in the clinical setting and thus have less continuity with student learning. Chickerella and Lutz (1981) note further that evaluation of a student performance is more difficult since faculty do not consistently observe students in the clinical area. Yet, even though faculty have experienced problems when using clinical preceptors, the positive aspects of the experience have outweighed the difficulties.

## ⋇ Advantages for the Preceptors

Health care providers have also reported that they receive benefits from working as clinical preceptors. In our own experience, clinical preceptors who have worked with us have stated that precepting is an important source of professional stimulation. These preceptors say that students keep them "on their toes" by asking questions, push them out of professional "ruts" by challenging the status quo, and present new ideas for managing longstanding health problems of chronic clients. One clinical preceptor at a community agency purposely assigns a client with longstanding health problems to the student to gain fresh insights and ideas on how to update the nursing care plan.

Students can further benefit clinical preceptors by creating incentives for the preceptor to pursue continuing education for the purpose of providing up-to-date care. Chickerella and Lutz (1981) and Clark (1981) report that staff nurses enjoy being clinical preceptors because the experience improves their own knowledge and skills, and allows them to demonstrate leadership and teaching skills.

Adams (1980) notes that another advantage gained from precepting as reported by nurses working as clinical preceptors was the increased input nurses had into care that was given to "their" patients by students. The nurses stated that the continuity of care was also increased when student and preceptor were responsible for providing care to the same group of patients. Another benefit of precepting reported by these nurses was their affiliation with academia. The nurses enjoyed having input into the teaching/learning process of the student. Osterweis, Chickodonz, Huntley, and Spencer (1980) found that nurses enjoyed precepting because they were involved in shaping details of teaching programs. Clark (1981) reported that preceptors simply enjoyed having an association with an academic setting.

According to Adams (1980), agencies have also benefited from pre-cepting. Agencies' staff reported that precepting provided an increased knowledge of course objectives and a mechanism for more input to faculty about student performance and about agency frustrations with academia. Both of these inputs were regarded as advantageous to the agency.

However, health care providers also experienced some frustration as clinical preceptors. Precepting students takes time. Clinical preceptors in general state that students require much time and support in providing nursing care to clients. However, on very busy days, clinical preceptors have very little time to give students, and this causes frustration for both preceptor and student (Adams, 1980; Chickerella & Lutz, 1981; Ferguson & Hauf, 1973; Osterweis et al., 1980). In our own experience, we have noted that in clinical settings the increased time demand of precepting students caused decreased client flow, which created problems for the preceptor and frustration for the clinic staff. The solution to this problem requires active, open communication among staff, preceptor and faculty to air complaints and provide continuous support to one another. Still, though time limitations are difficult to resolve, generally the positive re-turns from using preceptors far outweigh the frustrations.

## ENHANCED MUTUAL UNDERSTANDING BETWEEN EDUCATION AND SERVICE

As we have noted, there has historically been a rift between nursing education and nursing service. When nursing education moved to the ac-ademic setting and former clinical instructors were no longer qualified to teach, nurses had two avenues for advancement: (1) more education with an emphasis on teaching in the academic setting, or (2) more clinical and administrative experience in the practice setting. Thus, the original rift between education and service was widened. In the mid 1960s, factors such as the initiation of the primary nurse concept, a shift in nursing master's degree programs to include nurse clinicians, the emergence of the nurse practitioner role in the community, and the adoption of the nursing process began to improve professionalism in nursing care (Mauksch, 1980).

However, there remains an attitudinal gulf between nurses who give care and nurses who teach, and students are often caught in the middle of the political struggle between service providers and educators (Christman, 1979). Mauksch (1980) proposes that, as faculty recognize the increased clinical competence and professionalism of service providers, and as service pro-viders recognize the competence and expertise of faculty who are involved in practice and clinical research, the gap between education and service will begin to narrow. We ourselves have witnessed, along with Adams (1980), that the close association between educators and service providers fostered by use of qualified clinical preceptors has enhanced understanding between education and service.

The growing mutual understanding between education and service has largely been due to increased communication, a building of mutual trust and respect, and a close working relationship between faculty and service providers. These factors have helped students to attain clinical learning objectives.

## Increased Communication

The use of clinical preceptors has increased communication among faculty, service providers, and students in their efforts to standardize, monitor, and evaluate student clinical experiences. Communication is facilitated through orientation conferences where faculty review course objectives, course content and teaching plans with preceptors and students. Communication is also facilitated as faculty monitor the preceptorship to make sure learning objectives are being met. During this time faculty can facilitate communication between student and preceptor and provide guidance and support to the preceptor in meeting student learning needs through telephone conversations, periodic site visits, and planned conferences. Communication is again facilitated as faculty and service provider meet periodically to evaluate student performance and the preceptorship experience.

## Mutual Trust and Respect

When using a clinical preceptor, faculty and preceptor share responsibility for client care. The ultimate goal for both faculty and preceptor is to meet the health needs of the client through the best possible and most appropriate health care the student can deliver. As faculty and preceptor begin to grow in their relationship as partners in student learning, they also begin to build mutual trust and respect (Clark, 1981; Walters, 1981).

In our own experiences as faculty, as we began to recognize and respect the clinical knowledge and competence of qualified clinical preceptors, we noted that the clinical preceptors began to reciprocate respect by requesting assistance in selecting learning experiences, understanding student abilities, and clarifying their own responsibilities. Thus, together with other faculty (Adams, 1980; Clark, 1981), we have established a basis of mutual trust and respect with clinical preceptors. As we have gained more visibility and credibility in the health care community through close association with clinical preceptors, and as the mutual trust and respect have grown, the attitudinal gulf between the nurses who give care (the clinical preceptors) and the nurses who teach (the faculty) has narrowed.

## A Closer Working Relationship

The understanding between education and service is clearly enhanced when faculty work closely with qualified clinical preceptors. Yet, a major obstacle in improved understanding between education and service often arises when faculty select agencies for clinical learning sites. Faculty feel that educational standards are often compromised due to the inadequate learning experiences at many agencies. In one study, faculty from baccalaureate programs reported a willingness to make certain compromises in choosing agencies in order to provide enough learning sites for students (Hawkins, 1980). These compromises were made in the face of hostile attitudes in the agency toward students, poor communication between staff and faculty, poor continuity of care in the agency, poor quality of patient care in the agency, lack of good role models in the agency, conflicting professional philosophies between the agency and the educational program, unreceptiveness of the agency to student and faculty suggestions for change, and poor personnel policies in the agency. We believe, however, that, by working closely with qualified preceptors in agencies, faculty can avoid many of the compromises educators make in selecting agencies for clinical experiences.

A close working relationship with a clinical preceptor promotes communication between faculty and staff, which in turn fosters a more accepting atmosphere for student learning. In sharing responsibility for student performance, faculty and preceptor work together in making sure students deliver high quality health care that meets American Nurses' Association standards. Selection of a qualified preceptor also ensures that students will have appropriate role modeling of professional nursing interventions. A clinical preceptor selected according to qualifying criteria will have a professional philosophy that is congruent with the philosophy of the nursing program.

In our work, we have found that an agency is more likely to be receptive to student suggestions for change when the student has first identified the need along with the faculty and then discussed the need with the clinical preceptor. Change may be even more likely to occur if the student identifies the need along with the preceptor and both decide on possible solutions. It is important to note that, even though faculty and preceptor share responsibility for student learning, the faculty has ultimate responsibility for student learning.

**Summary**

Clearly, the use of clinical preceptors in nursing education programs has enhanced understanding between education and service. Because of the increased communication, mutual trust and respect, and close working relationship that faculty and preceptor enjoy, the preceptor gains a better understanding of educational goals and is thus able to provide relevant input into decisions regarding current needs in service settings. Adams (1980) states that, with the feedback and suggestions faculty obtain from preceptors at the end of the course, faculty can make changes in the course to strengthen the preceptor role and to enhance the learning environment of the student. By using qualified clinical preceptors, both education and service can more closely reach their mutual goal of providing consistent, quality client care.

## MAINTENANCE OF NURSING EDUCATION STANDARDS

It is important that criteria be established for the selection of qualified clinical preceptors. When developing a preceptorship experience, it is necessary to keep in mind that faculty hold ultimate responsibility for the quality of the educational experiences of students. Faculty can provide a quality clinical experience through a preceptor by providing a mechanism for standardizing, monitoring, and evaluating the preceptorships.

### Criteria for Selecting a Qualified Clinical Preceptor

The use of clinical preceptors has been successful in both nursing and medical education programs. The following criteria for selection of a qualified clinical preceptor are derived from studies done by the medical profession regarding qualities that make a preceptor effective, from experiences of faculty in nursing educational programs, and from our own experiences.

First of all, it is important that a preceptor portray a health care philosophy congruent with that of the educational program. Hawkins (1980) states that student philosophies of professional practice are often compromised when basic philosophical discrepancies exist between the agency in which the student practices and the educational program in which the student is enrolled. Thus it is important that a preceptor believe in and provide the quality of health care that is congruent with the educational program objectives.

Another important attribute of the preceptor that is cited in the literature and that we have also identified in our own work is enthusiasm for teaching.

Pietroni (1981) and Chickerella and Lutz (1981) have found that the most effective preceptors have a real enthusiasm for teaching. As health care providers, they like to, are able to, and are willing to take time to teach. Student learning is enhanced when a preceptor incorporates flexibility in the daily schedule to allow review of clients between client visits or at the end of the day. Some researchers of clinical preceptor effectiveness have noted the following preceptor attributes as contributing most to student learning in a preceptorship: The preceptor has a positive attitude toward the students and clients, allows the students to participate in providing health care, and emphasizes the problem-solving process rather than simple recall when teaching (Cotsonas & Kaiser, 1963; Stritter et al., 1975).

Another critical criterion in the selection of a preceptor is effectiveness as a health care provider. It is imperative that, as a role model, the preceptor have the experience, confidence and skills to provide good, quality health care (Adams, 1980; Chickerella & Lutz, 1981; Clark, 1981; Walters, 1981). In addition, the preceptor must be able to portray a commitment to meeting the health needs of clients. Part of this commitment includes consistent involvement in continuing education to keep up to date with current health care techniques and management of health problems. To further foster current management of health problems, it is important that updated, classic, relevant literature be accessible by the preceptor and student at the clinical site (Pietroni, 1981; Stritter et al., 1975).

When selecting a preceptor, the appropriateness of the clinical practice site for student learning is also an important consideration. It is essential that a broad range of clinical experiences be available at the practice site to fulfill educational objectives (Mentink et al., 1980).

Finally, in developing a preceptorship experience, it is important for the faculty to prepare the student carefully for the experience. The faculty of one program using preceptors found that the quality of the student learning experience was improved when the faculty assisted the students to be more self-directive and provided opportunities for the students to attain educational objectives through increased independent study (Ferguson & Hauf, 1973).

## Standardizing, Monitoring, and Evaluating the Preceptorship

One way of providing a quality preceptorship that is consistent with educational standards is to establish mechanisms that ensure facilitative communication between faculty and preceptor. Such mechanisms should allow for standardizing, monitoring, and evaluating the preceptorship. A mechanism used by many educational programs to standardize the preceptorship experience is an orientation conference or workshop for faculty, preceptor, and student. The purpose of the orientation is to make sure that the faculty, preceptor and student have a thorough understanding of the course objectives, an overall familiarity with the course content, and a knowledge of the responsibilities that each must assume. Some programs also encourage group development of teaching plans at such conferences (Adams, 1980; Chickerella & Lutz, 1981; Clark, 1981; DeMers, Lawrence, LoGerfo, Callen, Felton, Lester, & McCann, 1975; Ferguson & Hauf, 1973).

Mechanisms for monitoring and evaluating are necessary for continuous identification of student learning needs, evaluation of student progress, and evaluation of the general effectiveness of the preceptorship. Faculty are able to monitor student progress through daily logs, telephone contacts, and periodic conferences with preceptor and student. Further evaluation can be done through chart audits, observation of student clinical behavior, written examinations, and written evaluations of the experience by both student and preceptor (Adams, 1980; Chickerella & Lutz, 1981; DeMers et al., 1975; Walters, 1981). During the monitoring and evaluation phase, it is important for the preceptor to feel comfortable in discussing with faculty members student learning needs, possible student clinical experiences, and the preceptor's own needs and frustrations. Active communication is mandatory between preceptor, student and faculty to develop and maintain a successful learning relationship. It is also important to plan the preceptorship experience well in advance to allow for optimal preparation of each participant.


## CONCLUSION

Many nurse educators have found that the use of carefully selected, qualified clinical preceptors has greatly benefited students, faculty, and preceptors when the experience was standardized, monitored, and evaluated to uphold educational standards. Students have gained quality learning experiences with individualized attention from role models who were active practitioners. Faculty were able to focus on individual student needs in applying theory to practice and had more time to pursue their own practice, research, consultation, and publications. Preceptors experienced professional stimulation, had more input into the student care of "their" patients, and had more input into the educational process. Still, some special problems have been identified by educators and service providers. Faculty have found that the preceptorship experience demanded much time to coordinate effectively and afforded less continuity in following student learning. Preceptors have found that precepting students places great demands of time on their often busy schedules. However, the problems experienced were far outweighed by the benefits received.

Generally, the use of clinical preceptors helps to decrease the gap between education and service by enhancing understanding and mutual trust and respect between nurse providers and nurse educators. Both education and service are better able to reach their mutual goal of providing consistent, quality health care to clients.

The concept of using clinical preceptors in nursing education may have important implications for the future of the nursing profession:

- With the cost of nursing education spiraling continually upward, the use of clinical preceptors would enable nursing programs to prepare more students with fewer faculty. Use of preceptors would also provide ongoing, quality clinical learning experiences for students.

- Several authors in the nursing literature believe that nursing will become established and gain credibility as a clinical profession when nurses assume education, service, research, and consultation as integral parts of their professional role (Christman, 1979; Mauksch, 1980). The use of clinical preceptors allows more time for faculty to expand their academic role and mandates that preceptors expand their service role. Thus, the use of clinical preceptors could encourage and even necessitate more continuing education involvement by practicing nurses, more quality practitioners of nursing, and more clinical research by practicing faculty.

- A major trend in nursing education literature is for educators who are preparing practitioners to be practitioners themselves (Christman, 1979; Helmuth & Guberski, 1980; Mauksch, 1980; Nayer, 1980; Rauen, 1974; Reiter, 1966; Sherman, 1980). The use of clinical preceptors would afford more time for faculty to pursue their own clinical practice; as faculty establish their own practice, they can also precept students. Rauen (1974) has suggested that faculty preceptors could increase the effectiveness of nursing education and increase student satisfaction.

- The use of mentors in nursing deserves careful consideration in future development and implementation of preceptorships (Hamilton, 1981). Historically, mentors have provided an honorable means for helping a neophyte develop, often postgraduation, in a profession. Although the specifics of design and implementation are different for each, the underlying premises for the use of mentors and preceptors are similar with regard to applying theory to practice in the real world.

Generally, we believe that the use of clinical preceptors can enhance the nursing profession by bridging the education-service gap, by encouraging nurse educators and nurse providers to assume all components of the professional role, by enhancing student learning satisfaction, and by providing better overall health care to patients.

## REFERENCES

Adams, D.E. Agency staff facilitate student learning. *Nursing Outlook,* 1980, *28*(6), 382–385.

Chickerella, B.C., & Lutz, W.J. Professional nurturance: Preceptorships for undergraduate nursing students. *American Journal of Nursing,* 1981, *81*(1), 107–109.

Christman, L. The practitioner-teacher. *Nurse Educator,* 1979, *18,* 8–11.

Clark, M.D. Staff nurses as clinical teachers. *American Journal of Nursing,* 1981, *81*(2), 314–318.

Cotsonas, N.J., & Kaiser, H.F. Student evaluation of clinical teaching. *Journal of Medical Education,* 1963, *38,* 742–745.

Crancer, J.; Fournier, M.; & Maury-Hess, S. Clinical practicum before graduation. *Nursing Outlook,* 1975, *23*(2), 99–102.

DeMers, J.L.; Lawrence, D.M.; LoGerfo, J.P.; Callen, W.; Felton, H.; Lester, K.; & McCann, B. Standardizing, monitoring, evaluating preceptorships: A model for decentralized medical education. *Journal of Medical Education,* 1975, *50,* 471–473.

Ferguson, M., & Hauf, B. The preceptor role: Implementing student experience in community nursing (Parts 1 and 2). *Journal of Continuing Education in Nursing,* 1973, *4*(1), 13–16; *4*(5), 14–16.

Friedman, C.P.; Baker, R.M.; & Paige, E. Functions of a family medicine preceptorship. *Journal of Medical Education,* 1979, *54,* 567–574.

Hall, M.B. How do students learn on a primary nursing care unit? *Nursing Outlook,* 1977, *25*(6), 370–373.

Hamilton, M.S. Mentorhood: A key to nursing leadership. *Nursing Leadership,* 1981, *4*(1), 4–13.

Harris, D.L., & Blum, H.P. An evaluation of primary care preceptorships. *Journal of Family Practice,* 1977, *5*(4), 577–579.

Hawkins, J.W. Selections of clinical agencies for baccalaureate nursing education. *Journal of Nursing Education,* 1980, *19*(8), 7–17.

Helmuth, M.R., & Guberski, T.D. Preparation for preceptor role. *Nursing Outlook,* 1980, *28*(1), 36–39.

Mahr, D.R. RN preceptors: Do they help students? *AORN Journal,* 1979, *30*(4), 724–730.

Malkemes, L.C. Resocialization: A model for nurse practitioner preparation. *Nursing Outlook,* 1974, *22*(2), 90–94.

Mauksch, I.G. Faculty practice: A professional imperative. *Nurse Educator,* 1980, *5*(3), 21–24.

Mentink, J.L.; Trolinger, J.; & O'Hara-Devereaux, M. Nurse practitioners in primary care. *Family and Community Health,* 1980, *3*(2), 35–48.

Nayer, D.D. Unification: Bringing nursing service and nursing education together. *American Journal of Nursing,* 1980, *80*(6), 1112–1113.

Osterweis, M.; Chickodonz, G.; Huntley, R.R.; & Spencer, D.C. HMO development for primary care team teaching of medical and nursing students. *Journal of Medical Education,* 1980, *55*(9), 743–750.

Pietroni, P.C. Community office experience for family medicine residents. *Journal of Medical Education,* 1981, *56,* 43–49.

Rauen, K.C. The clinical instructor as role model. *Journal of Nursing Education,* 1974, *13,* 33–40.

Reiter, F.K. The clinical nursing approach. *Nursing Forum,* 1966, *5*(1), 40–44.

Sherman, J.E. Role modeling for FNP students. *Nursing Outlook,* 1980, *28,* 40–42.

Skinner, S.R., & Rogers, K.D. A medical student organized and directed primary care preceptorship. *Journal of Medical Education,* 1974, *49,* 1145–1151.

Stritter, F.T.; Hain, J.D.; & Grimes, D.A. Clinical teaching re-examined. *Journal of Medical Education,* 1975, *50,* 876–882.

Sultz, H.A.; Zielezny, M.; & Kinyon, L. *Longitudinal study of nurse practitioners* (U.S. DHEW Publication Number [HRA] 76–43). Washington, D.C.: U.S. Government Printing Office, 1976.

Taylor, J. Genesis of the nurse practitioner role. *Occupational Health Nursing,* 1975, *23*(8), 15–17.

Walters, C.R. Using staff preceptors in a senior experience. *Nursing Outlook,* 1981, *29*(4), 245–247.

Wilson, H.S.; Vaughan, H.C.; & Gaff, J.G. The second step model of baccalaureate education for registered nurses: The student's perspective. *Journal of Nursing Education,* 1977, *16,* 27–34.

# Chapter 3

# How To Select Preceptors

*Sandra Stuart-Siddall*

The process by which a faculty member or representative from a nursing program locates and selects a preceptor is relatively simple. In fact, though we treat the utilization of preceptors as something new in nursing education, it actually is an activity that is merely "coming out of the closet." Public health nurses (PHNs) who share their case loads, desks, and cars one-to-one with eager student nurses (SNs) have been preceptoring for years in nursing education. Although those PHNs were not then called preceptors, we now recognize them as such. Indeed, we can further broaden the definition of the word to encompass other clinical supervisors who have student contacts in the vast array of nursing specialties.

## THE SELECTION PROCESS

As in all systems there are hierarchies in nursing service and nursing education. Someone in the nursing educational institution must accept the responsibility of defining the course content through which preceptor-based education is seen to be an asset in the curriculum. That same faculty person will want to demonstrate the need for the preceptorship course and to prepare a presentation for the dean or chairperson of the school of nursing.

For the majority of nurse educators or educators in related health fields, the following process would be applicable in initiating a preceptorship in a curriculum: A nursing faculty member approaches the dean or chairperson to discuss the need for preceptors in the course the faculty member is teaching. The dean or chairperson will then either (1) decide that the proposal is appropriate and give the go-ahead to pursue the activity or (2) request the faculty person to prepare a presentation for the next faculty meeting. In the presentation the faculty person should answer the following questions:

- In which course will the preceptors be utilized?
- How will the use of preceptors improve the course?
- How will the preceptors be selected?
- What criteria will be used to select the preceptors?
- From which facilities will the preceptors be chosen?
- What will be the role and responsibility of the preceptors?

The courses in which preceptors are used are generally upper division courses, since SNs are close to graduation or at the very least a senior or a junior going into the senior year. The courses are typically identified as independent studies, senior level practicum, nursing trends, or elective courses in which a nursing specialty is studied.

The ways in which preceptors can improve such a course are becoming more evident: Reality orientation in education, working one-to-one with a clinical preceptor, gives the SN an opportunity to work in the real world of nursing, with a buddy, but still protects the SN under the aegis of academia. Most traditional or nonpreceptor experiences have so many constraints, limitations, guidelines, rules, client selectivity controls, and census or case load controls that the student does not get a feel for the real, day-to-day world of nursing. In the formative period, those early stages in which a new student nurse is adjusting to the curriculum and the course work and working with real patients, these protective controls are necessary for the SN, the faculty, and the client. However, as the SN nears graduation, more independence is needed.

A program of nursing that does not build into the curriculum a preceptorship is flawed. From the preceptorship experience, the SN will gain increased confidence and self-reliance and become more manually adept at a variety of nursing treatments and nursing assessments. Furthermore, the shocks, pleasures, disappointments, paperwork, and bureaucratic processes found in day-to-day work are all there for the student to experience firsthand—not screened or buffered by faculty or one-quarter or one-half day clinical time, which is a definite constraint on reality learning.

## PROBLEMS

Once the faculty have an opportunity to hear how their colleague intends to use the preceptor, all is not necessarily going to go smoothly. There are still nursing faculty who feel threatened by the use of preceptors. They see the use of this particular educational model as resulting in a loss of power over their students and as producing problems with quality control and control over what is happening with their SNs in the clinical setting. They may view the preceptor as a threat to their very purpose at their institute—to teach.

The proponents of preceptors can only regard such resistance with frustration and sadness. Educators who have used preceptors have, in fact, found that when selected with care they amplify the student's learning experience. In other words, the quality of a clinical experience improves. This is especially true in a nursing specialty where the clinician is current in skill and technique while the nursing faculty is current in theory and knowledge, but not in skill. What better way to present an educational experience to a student than to combine the best of two worlds—education and the knowledge and theory underlying it with nursing service and its associated skills and technical competencies?

Under the guidance of a clinical preceptor, the student must function under specific academic guidelines or a written behavioral objective contract. To the degree the SN adopts the expected behaviors, the evaluation of the SN for grade assignment will be facilitated.

Even after years of reading educational journal discussions of grading and evaluation processes, it is not uncommon to find faculty still floundering at midterm or at the end of the term. The problem is usually that, without specific guidelines and objectives, the instructor cannot issue an objective grade. When there are objective guidelines to follow, in contrast, there is no loss of control over the experience; in fact more objective control results. Everybody knows what is expected and how to proceed to gain or meet the expected outcomes: evaluating and grading for the instructor, directing activities and learning experiences at a selected pace for the SN, and providing guidelines for selection of clients and situations to help meet academic objectives for the preceptor.

In such a situation, will the faculty person lose control over the SN? Perhaps. But taking into consideration that over several years thousands of pages of reading, hundreds of hours of instruction, and hundreds of hours of clinical work have in theory prepared the SN for independence, self-direction, and an ability to gain firsthand experience in the real work world of the nurse, faculty persons would clearly be remiss if they failed to place students in a self-directed, clinically saturated academic course prior to graduation. Yet, SNs are still graduating without having worked a full eight-hour shift, without having made any decisions for patient care and treatment during that shift, without having handled personnel conflicts, and without having prioritized what to do for a full load of patients/clients—

8 to 12 patients as opposed to the 2 to 4 patients an SN is typically assigned throughout many nursing programs right up to graduation.

As for the threat to the very purpose of being a professor or instructor, only self-analysis and self-confrontations, with questions like, "What really is the bottom line of my resistance to using a preceptor?" will bring this feeling to the surface. Once the feeling is identified, the process to deal with it can begin. A very efficacious way to deal with this perceived threat is to learn about the actual use of preceptors. Teaching for teaching's sake is useless and wasteful; there must be creative approaches to teaching and use of teaching time. All of us in nursing education need more time for self-improvement, keeping current in our nursing field, committee work, professional writing, test development, test grading, counseling students, preparing lectures, and so on. By using preceptorships appropriately, an instructor can in fact free up extra time to be more effective in all these areas, and thus make the educational process for a soon-to-graduate nurse more oriented toward reality. If a student has a poor educational experience, it reflects on the institute and the instructor; that surely is more of a threat to teaching ability than the fostering of independence and confidence by releasing a student to a preceptor.

## IMPLEMENTATION

Once the majority of the faculty agree to the use of preceptors, the practical work of implementation can begin. In choosing a person to function as a preceptor, the place to begin is with the upper management of the health institution. If the facility has students or staff who have served as preceptors before, or it is a facility currently being used by the educator for clinical placements, half of the work is already done. With the green light from the administration regarding the use of SNs in the facility, efforts can now be focused on:

- explaining the philosophy of the nursing program
- detailing the objectives of the course for which the preceptorship is intended
- describing the safeguards and legalities built into the experience, discussing the responsibilities of each participant
- identifying the times when the SNs are in the facility
- projecting numbers of potential SNs per semester
- exploring with the administrative staff some of their expectations and feelings about having SNs working with the staff

- outlining typical time commitments a staff person might have with an SN assignment
- describing typical situations that might arise with SNs working in the facility under the guidance of a preceptor
- defining the role of a preceptor
- providing a schematical diagram of the communication channels between the educator, the SN, the preceptor, the director of the nursing service (DNS) and the administrator.

Much of this information can be put in writing, organized in a small folder or booklet for the administration to keep. Listening to the educator and asking questions can result in an effective exchange of information, but having a booklet to read afterwards, to digest the information that was transferred back and forth, is more conducive to ultimate decision making and understanding.

## CRITERIA

Once the administration agrees to have SNs in the facility and to provide the educator with access to the staff for use as preceptors, the next step is to talk to the DNS of the facility. The DNS can elaborate on the information already collected. On this basis, the screening process can begin to find out who would function best as a preceptor. At some institutions, when staff people hear about the need for preceptors, they will volunteer their services—as opposed to being approached and asked to volunteer. In the majority of cases, however, the DNS will provide the educator with a list of names of staff people who, for a variety of reasons, are likely candidates for a preceptor role. The following are some of the criteria a DNS would take into consideration in selecting staff nurses as preceptors:

- educational background
- functional level as a nurse
- attitude about having SNs in the facility
- role-modeling ability
- supervisory skills
- communication abilities
- attitude about nursing
- ability to cope with stress
- understanding of the facility's philosophies and policies
- rapport with other staff.

By applying these criteria to the staff list, the likely candidates will become apparent. With this list of candidates, the educator will continue the screening process.

Up to this point, the educator has engaged the following areas in the hierarchy: (1) the dean or director of the candidate's program of nursing, (2) the colleagues or team teachers in the same program, (3) the administrator of the health facility to be used, and (4) the DNS of that facility. Because this is an academic experience and one in which the SN is entrusted, under specific guidelines, to work independently with a preceptor, the educator now has to combine the educator's own criteria with the DNS's criteria, to single out the primary preceptors.

The Board of Registered Nursing, the National League of Nursing, private consultants, faculty, deans and directors all have views as to what a person needs to have as a basic background to assist in teaching student nurses on the clinical level. According to the *Laws Relating to Nursing Education-Licensure-Practice with Rules and Regulations Manual* issued by the California Board of Registered Nursing (1980) "a clinical teaching assistant shall work only in clinical teaching areas and under the direction of an instructor and shall have had at least five years in the practice of professional nursing in the clinical area to which he/she is assigned" (section 1427[5]). This is the basic legal requirement for a preceptor in California. Any additional requirements are identified and defined by the facility DNS and/or the educator. The criteria an educator may develop in addition to those already identified in the selection of potential preceptors might include these attributes of the staff person:

- previous or past experience with SNs
- use of a preceptor with the staff person as a student
- "gut" feelings about working with students
- highest level of education, the BSN- and MSN-prepared nurse being most desirable
- how the staff person teaches, using examples or role modeling
- interests in education
- personality
- current workload (would a student assignment overtax the staff person?)
- knowledge and skill level within the staff person's nursing specialty
- pursuit of continuing education credit in the staff person's nursing specialty
- willingness to participate in evaluative type activities to assist the educator in grading the student

- understanding of the purposes, focus, and goals of the course under which the SN is doing the preceptorship
- agreement to work with behavioral objective contracts or related academic paperwork
- commitment to higher education and/or nursing education
- reaction to the need to plan and evaluate the learning episode
- ability to let the SN discover self and to foster self-reliance and self-initiated inquiry.

## CONCLUSION

Nursing students have a variety of backgrounds, interests, abilities and personalities. The educator's ability to match a preceptor with a given SN will be a measure of the success of the educator's efforts. It is possible that, since a preceptor functions mainly as a role model, supervisor, and facilitator in the nursing course, the educator may wish to utilize RNs exclusively. Physicians, nurse practitioners, and physician assistants can function very well as preceptors. Nursing students have little trouble separating these roles from that of nursing.

Also, if a baccalaureate nurse is not available to serve in your facility of choice, the educator may wish to select the nurse who best fits the rest of the criteria. There are thousands of diploma and associate degree nurses in the work force today. By virtue of their clinical specialty and experience, they too make very fine preceptors. An overemphasis on the preceptor being a baccalaureate-prepared nurse will severely limit the multitude of stimulating and exciting educational opportunities available in preceptorship courses.

**REFERENCE**

California Board of Registered Nursing. *Laws relating to nursing education-licensure-practice with rules and regulations manual.* Sacramento, Calif.: Department of Consumer Affairs, Board of Registered Nursing, 1980.

# Chapter 4

# How To Design a Course Based on a Preceptor Experience

*Elaine Elizabeth Dye-White*

In an attempt to resolve the dilemmas that exist between the "ideal" world of nursing education and the "real" world of nursing practice in light of the increased demand for nurses in rural areas, many nursing programs are placing students in rural settings, using preceptors for student supervision. The use of preceptor faculty supervision in a rural setting also serves to expand and diversify the learning experiences and to provide rural preceptor role models for nursing students.

At the baccalaureate level, faculty at California State University, Long Beach, a public-supported, urban institution, are using rural-based preceptors to resolve the dilemmas we have noted. The rural placement program has evolved in response to two trends in community health nursing education: (1) clinical placements increasingly focused upon clinic practice with diminishing opportunities for home visiting, family evaluation, family teaching, and community interaction; and (2) a growing desire on the part of faculty and students to become more involved in the rural setting. The rural setting provides unique opportunities for the student to develop interdependent nursing roles, problem-solving skills, and critical thinking abilities. This experience allows the student to become involved in the community, to plan for care, and to intervene realistically in the community to provide care. Another positive outcome is that students are assisted to identify other areas of nursing practice that are not in urban, highly technological settings but are just as fulfilling and demanding. Persons serving as preceptors in rural areas have much to offer students in applying theory, research, and new concepts to intervention in rural nursing practice. These preceptors are experts in their field and serve as practicing role models.

## STUDENTS

The student population at California State University, Long Beach, reflects lower-, middle-, and upper-class social strata and represents many ethnocultural groups. The students we have found to benefit most from a rural placement with a preceptor are those in their final year of clinical nursing. These students may be registered nurses who have completed a diploma or associate degree program and are working toward a baccalaureate, or they may be generic students with no prior nursing education or experience. They are typically older and bring to the educational setting a unique blend of life experience and past education that demands an alteration or modification of the traditional senior year nursing clinical and theory work. These students have mastered the technical, bedside nursing skills and are ready to assimilate the professional nursing role into their repertoire of practice. They have the ability to solve problems, to think critically and logically, and to apply and use the nursing process in their practice. They have a background in pathophysiology, psychosocial cultural assessment, physical assessment, natural and social sciences, and nursing theory.

When the program at Long Beach first began, students selecting the rural option were placed in rural settings according to their areas of interest. As the program evolved, some students benefited from the program and some did not. After evaluation of the program by nursing faculty, preceptor faculty, and students, two major factors were identified as affecting the outcome of the learning experience: (1) the students' ability to adapt quickly to new situations, and (2) their ability to work independently and interdependently. Some students were very interested in the rural nursing experience but, when faced with living in a rural community and a foreign environment and interacting with indigenous community members on a professional, day-to-day basis, found themselves unable to cope with the new situation and thus benefited little from the rural experience.

Students must cope in this new rural environment without the immediate emotional support of their family and friend support systems, and, initially, they often experience feelings of loneliness and isolation. A support network is provided through the use of preceptors and indigenous community persons to assist the students in coping with feelings of isolation and loneliness.

## CURRICULUM

The nursing curriculum offered at the California State University at Long Beach is an integrated one. The generic curriculum is based upon a foundation in the natural and social sciences. The first year consists of nursing skills, pharmacology, nutrition, legal aspects, and psychosocial cultural assessment. The second year of clinical nursing consists of the nursing process applied to the functional areas of medical surgical nursing, obstetrics, pediatrics, psychiatric nursing, physical assessment, and growth and development through the life span.

The registered nurse student curriculum builds upon the student's curriculum that led to licensure. Students must have completed courses equivalent to those required of the generic students in the natural and social sciences and must complete one year of clinical nursing, which includes nursing process theory, physical assessment, psychosociocultural assessment, and growth and development through the life span. The one year of clinical nursing courses must be completed prior to the senior year.

In the senior year, the generic and the registered nurse groups are blended together to complete the senior year courses. The senior year stresses nursing care in an ambulatory setting, with increased attention to illness prevention and health teaching concepts. The goal is to develop the ability to function as a professional independently and interdependently with other members of the health team. Skills in consultation and collaboration with other health team members are developed. The two semester courses are designed so that the experiences gained in the first semester serve as a foundation for the second semester. Because ambulatory care is accentuated, both semesters are very amenable to the use of preceptors in rural and urban settings.

The first semester of the senior year is a blend of organized learning experiences in urban official and nonofficial agencies monitored by clinical instructors and preceptors. Students in this semester are introduced to the public health nurse role and function in this role with the assistance of the instructor. The students gain experience in official health agencies and, in addition, experience the public health nursing role in other settings. The nonofficial agency settings include the Visiting Nurse Association, home health agencies, public and private schools, community-based organizations (both public and private) that provide health services to unwed mothers, and groups of senior citizens, the disabled, and the poor. In the first semester, the students are guided in their growth from dependent, interdependent learners to learners who are independent and interdependent. The course stresses the interdependent role and begins to develop independent learning and nursing skills. Skills are developed in realistic self-evaluation to identify cognitive, affective, and psychomotor strengths and weaknesses and the ability to identify learning experiences to strengthen weak areas.

The second semester of the course places emphasis upon development of interdependent and independent learning skills and nursing practice. In this semester, the students are offered the opportunity to work further in their "areas of concentration." These areas are selected ambulatory settings and include geriatrics, critical care, community mental health, obstetrics, neonatology, pediatrics, administration, and community health nursing in urban and rural settings. The content areas in seminars encompass (1) psychosocial cultural factors and their influence on individual and family responses to changes in health status, (2) theories of teaching and learning applied to groups and individuals, (3) current management of specific health problems, and (4) application of research to nursing practices.

Because of the diverse options offered, the efficacy of preceptors to monitor the experience and serve as role models is obvious. In the second semester, the students confer with their instructor in order to agree mutually upon an area of concentration and are offered suggestions as to possible field placements that will meet the students' learning needs. Most of these field placements have already been initially contacted and evaluated by the faculty as to their appropriateness. The students are encouraged to identify their own placements and to collaborate with personnel in those agencies in order to develop their own learning objectives and identify learning experiences that meet their individual needs.

For those students selecting community health nursing in a rural setting, additional screening is required. The rural community health program has developed a summary packet for faculty and students that identifies the goals and objectives of the program and provides a brief overview of the kinds of learning experiences available, a student application form, information regarding types of housing available, descriptions of the rural counties available for student placement, and information for faculty (for example, guidelines for rural clinical placement preceptors). The rural placement center identifies rural preceptors and agencies willing to provide learning experiences to community health nursing students. The nursing instructor meets individually with the students requesting rural placement and interviews them to identify their past learning experiences, current interests, ability to cope with new situations, and ability to work independently and interdependently. The faculty consult with other faculty in this process in order to identify those students who might not be suited for the experience but might instead be best suited for a placement in a community health urban setting.

The students are required to complete a daily or weekly log of their activities in the rural placement. They must also develop learning objectives and an evaluation tool to be completed by the rural placement preceptor at the end of the learning experience. The preceptor evaluates the students as to whether their learning objectives were met and at what level, using a Leikert-type ranking system. The evaluation tools and student logs are used by the nursing faculty in the determination of the students' course grades.

Using this type of curriculum as a model, it is clear that the first two years of nursing education, with its emphasis on technical, bedside nursing skills, are not appropriate for preceptor use. The first two years of clinical nursing (in the generic program), and the first year of clinical nursing (in the registered nurse program) provide the structure and specific learning experiences that emphasize the technical nurse role. The rural placement, with its emphasis upon independent and interdependent practice, builds upon the basic nursing knowledge and skills gained in these functional areas. For example, to function in a rural setting, the provision of care to a prenatal patient with other children requires that the student possess an understanding of obstetrics, pediatrics, growth and development, physical assessment, and, in many instances, concepts from psychiatric nursing. Concepts in these areas must be included in nursing intervention strategies and are often modified by the student to meet the unique needs of the student's clients in a rural setting. It is impossible to modify or change intervention strategies without a basic understanding of the functional areas of nursing. The use of preceptors does not allow for constant surveillance, guidance, and evaluation. The students are expected to evaluate their own levels of expertise and the needs of the client and family and then to consult with the preceptor as needed. Students more readily assume this level of functioning after their first two years of clinical nursing (for generic students) or their first year of clinical nursing (for registered nurse students).

## CONCLUSION

The integration of preceptors in the clinical (field) experience of baccalaureate student nurses has been a powerful means to expand the available number of placements, to bring students in contact with the real world, and, hopefully, to help them resolve contradictions between the "real" versus the "ideal" worlds. The experience also serves to provide the student with professional role models in rural settings and to kindle an interest in rural nursing.

This experience has been of great benefit to the preceptors because it assists them to become aware of current concepts in the nursing curriculum, to provide feedback to the instructor as to perceived student learning needs and possible content areas to be included in the curriculum. The integrated curriculum has been found most amenable to the use of rural preceptors.

The rural clinic experience is most beneficial to the students after they have completed the functional, technical areas of nursing and are able to integrate knowledge gained in those areas and apply it in new situations.

# Chapter 5

# How To Utilize a Preceptor

*Arlene Parrish Gray*

The effective use of a preceptor demands time and commitment of both the faculty and the preceptor. This chapter offers suggestions for establishing a preceptorship that will be mutually beneficial for the faculty, student, preceptor, and the consumer that is served.

## THE PROCESS

The phases or steps used to establish a preceptorship are similar to those utilized by the nurse in establishing a therapeutic relationship with a client. Wilson and Kneisl (1979) suggest the following three phases:

1. beginning or orientation phase when contact is established
2. middle or working phase when contact is maintained
3. end or termination phase when contact is evaluated and terminated.

### Establishing the Relationship

The goal of the first phase is to initiate contact with the preceptor. One of the first tasks is to clarify the purpose of the preceptorship and to identify the roles, responsibilities, and privileges of the preceptor, faculty, and student. Ideally, written information on the purpose of the preceptorship, the objectives of the clinical experience, and the expectations of the preceptor would be sent to the preceptor to review prior to the first conference with the faculty, at which time they could be elaborated upon. The first personal contact may be made at the agency to be utilized for the preceptorship. This may be done in a meeting in the preceptor's territory. Such a meeting may provide more security for a novice preceptor who may have misconceptions and fears about the experience. It also demonstrates an interest in the agency and its services and provides an opportunity for the faculty to become acquainted with the physical facilities, the philosophy and purposes of the agency, the services offered, the resources available, the role of the nurse in the setting, and other relevant aspects.

One of the most important steps in the first phase is to establish a trusting relationship with mutual understanding and respect between the faculty and preceptor. One of the ways to begin this process is to establish a common interest or bond. This may result from each sharing personal information, including information on past work and educational experiences. The issue of credibility may arise when clinical competence is questioned by either or both. Depending upon how the preceptor assesses the value of formal education, the faculty person may or may not be perceived as credible based on advanced educational preparation. On the other hand, it is essential for the faculty person to perceive the preceptor as a credible, valuable member of the educational team. The faculty person may wish to spend some time with the preceptor, observing the preceptor's normal role in the clinical setting and thus assist in building confidence in the competence of the preceptor.

When possible, it is useful for the faculty to demonstrate their own expertise to establish mutual credibility. The preceptors for their part must perceive themselves as contributing practical, reality-oriented perspectives to the student learning experience. The preceptorship experience thus is seen to be mutually beneficial to the student, preceptor, agency, and faculty. Each provides a stimulus for growth and learning.

As a part of the orientation to the preceptor role, the faculty should present an overview of the nursing curriculum, including the philosophy and objectives of the program, the specific course content and objectives in the affiliated course, and a description of how the clinical experience relates to classroom activities. This overview will provide better continuity between theory and application. The specific objectives of the preceptorship should be discussed and agreed upon. Roles, responsibilities, rights, and privileges should be identified for the preceptor, faculty person, and student.

In addition to the conference between the faculty and preceptor, a planning session with the student present may be held during the latter half of the meeting with the preceptor at the agency or at a subsequent time. Collaborative planning facilitates congruence between the requisite learning, the interests and needs of the student, and the available opportunities in the clinical area. This promotes a relevant and meaningful learning experience for the student, who tends to learn best when involved in selecting the learning experiences. At the joint meeting, each of the roles and responsibilities should be clarified. Mutual commitment is necessary to continue the process. However, provision to abort the plan must be made in the event one of the parties chooses not to continue with the preceptorship.

When mutual willingness is attained, an agreement or contract can be prepared. This may be a formal contract or a letter of agreement delineating the responsibilities of each party. Dates and time frames should be specified so that each is aware of the expectations and time commitments. The faculty, student, and preceptor each retain a copy of the signed agreement. If a formal contract is required by the parent agency, university, or health facility, advanced planning is necessary, since it may take months to obtain the approval of the individuals responsible for legal decisions.

Following the agency visit, it is useful to send a written communication to the preceptor, summarizing the substantive content and plans. This gives the preceptor an opportunity to respond to any misperceptions or misunderstandings that may have arisen. Thus, validation is accomplished.

The first phase of establishing the preceptor relationship provides the essential foundation on which the learning experience will develop. The mutual understanding and respect established during the first phase become essential tools for the second phase, maintaining the relationship.

**Maintaining the Relationship**

Once the preceptorship is operational, the working phase begins. In this second phase, the educational plan is implemented, with student learning as the main goal. The focus is on assisting the student to meet the designated clinical objectives. The student learning objectives provide the guideline for the experience. Written behavioral objectives describing the learning activities will assist in planning, implementing, and evaluating the learning experience. The objectives may include core objectives applicable to all students enrolled in the course, reflecting application of course content, as well as individual student objectives that serve to individualize the experience to meet unique student interests and needs. The individual student objectives may be written by the student with input from the faculty person.

The role of the preceptor during the second phase is to serve as a resource person, role model, and consultant to the assigned student. Role modeling is an effective teaching tool during this phase. The preceptor who is an excellent, expert clinician can demonstrate the application of nursing theory to nursing practice. The faculty person must provide opportunities to demonstrate the application of classroom theory in the clinical setting. Ideally, with assistance, the student will be able to integrate the theory from the educational setting into the real world. The insights that develop as a result of this synthesis may minimize future reality shock.

The primary role of the student during the second phase is that of learner, though the student also contributes to the agency's goals through the use of the nursing process with clients affiliated with the health care facility. The ultimate purpose of all professional health care behavior is to deliver quality care to clients, regardless of setting. All clinical activities should be directed toward this goal. In this way, learning becomes a means to an end rather than the end itself.

The faculty person is responsible for clinical supervision to maintain quality control during the working phase of the process. Indirect supervision is accomplished through periodic phone conversations with the preceptor, onsite agency visits, conversations with the student during regularly scheduled appointments, and student feedback in class and seminar. Written and oral assignments that demonstrate student understanding and the application of pertinent concepts and skills will validate the application of theory in the clinical area. A diary or log written by the student will provide additional documentation of what transpires during the clinical experience. However, the faculty person retains control of student evaluations and is responsible for assigning the appropriate grade. Input from both preceptor and student may assist in this process.

Occasionally during the second phase, problems may develop in the preceptorship. It may become evident that the planned clinical experience is not effectively meeting the designated objectives, for whatever reasons. In this situation, the role of the faculty is to ensure a quality learning experience for the student. Continuous evaluation is necessary to prevent or detect problems. Interventions should include communication with both the preceptor and the student to collect data to validate or invalidate concerns, should share observations and concerns with a focus on student learning, and should utilize the problem-solving process to explore possible solutions. A collaborative approach is usually the most effective technique in problem analysis and resolution. The rights and responsibilities of each must be kept in mind. The formal contract or agreement usually stipulates steps to be taken when a breach of contract occurs or termination is desired. An emphasis on thorough collaborative planning with consistent follow-up during the second phase will usually keep channels of communication open to prevent insurmountable problems. When each member of the team functions at a high level, the system works well.

It should be noted that the second phase, which focuses on the implementation of the student learning plan, is limited by time constraints that designate when the clinical experience should be terminated.

**Terminating the Relationship**

The objective of the final phase is the termination of the preceptor contact in a mutually planned and satisfying manner. The first task is the evaluation of the clinical experience. A conference between the preceptor, student, and faculty affords an opportunity to discuss positive and negative aspects, to determine goal achievement in relation to the clinical objectives, to identify methods to improve the experience, and to summarize the value of the experience for each participant. A part of the evaluation conference should be devoted to a debriefing session during which each person may review the experience from that person's own perspective. Sharing expectations, fears, insights, and learning is useful as each attempts to personalize the experience and provide closure.

A process or formative evaluation is continuous throughout the learning experience to indicate how learning is progressing. A product or summative evaluation is conducted at the end of the term, with outcomes evaluated in relation to course requirements. Grades are assigned by the faculty.

The second task in the termination phase is to discuss future plans for the preceptorship. If plans are indefinite, the faculty person may solicit the preceptor's continued interest in serving as a preceptor and thus pave the way for future negotiations. If the agency is not needed in the immediate future, the faculty person should inform the preceptor of that fact, express appreciation for participating in the learning experience, and suggest the possibility of future use.

In this connection, the faculty member must be aware of the risks involved in sporadic use of preceptors. The preceptor may lose interest in the preceptorship, may agree to serve as a preceptor for another educational institution, or may feel rejected and unneeded by the faculty and affiliated program. In any event, the preceptor may be unavailable for future use. If the faculty person wishes to continue the preceptorship in the following term, a discussion with the preceptor must be held to determine the feasibility and the preceptor's willingness to serve. A mutual agreement to that end must be reached, with specific plans delineated.

A letter of appreciation should be sent by the faculty to the preceptor, acknowledging the contribution made with a copy to the preceptor's immediate supervisor. Other types of recognition may be a certificate awarded the preceptor, an appointment to a university advisory council or other appropriate body, or possibly an appointment to adjunct faculty status. In any case, the faculty should acknowledge the preceptor's contribution in as many tangible ways as is possible, since the preceptor is not usually rewarded monetarily for participating.

In establishing a preceptorship, the faculty's role is critical in each phase. Self-awareness, with insight into one's own needs, values, beliefs, and biases is very helpful during the process. Helping skills that promote growth in self and others, strengthen available resources, and encourage responsibility and accountability are also important. Effective communication that demonstrates listening skills and emphasizes a problem-solving approach is an essential ingredient. The success of the preceptorship will depend greatly upon the skill shown by the faculty person in developing it.

## CONCERNS AND ISSUES

In utilizing a preceptor, several faculty concerns may emerge. A few of these will be discussed with suggestions for possible resolution.

### Control

The issue of control is faced by many faculty members involved in the preceptorship triad for the first time. Faculty have traditionally been socialized into the role of providing close and personal supervision of most clinical learning experiences. Many faculty receive gratification from nurturing the student in the clinical setting and take pride in how the student acquires new knowledge and skill with assistance from the faculty member. A feeling on the part of faculty members of being needed and valued may result. Thus, the faculty may feel unrewarded and unneeded when faced with the fact that they are not directly and continuously involved in the clinical setting. They may experience symptoms typically associated with loss.

The nurturing needs of the faculty may be met in a variety of ways. A redefinition of the teaching role may be in order to promote the concept of the educator as facilitator. It may be useful to perceive the student-faculty relationship as similar to that of the nurse-client helping relationship. The skills are the same, thus, the faculty may be shown to be rewarded by using those skills in any setting. Their gratification may come by evaluating the learning outcomes and taking pride in being a part of the learning process.

Many opportunities for input into the clinical experience present themselves during conferences with individual students, in class or seminar, and during onsite agency visits. Written feedback on class assignments also provides opportunities for direct involvement. Process or tape recording assignments offer excellent means for participating in the nurse-client interactions of the student. Because there is less opportunity for demonstrating nursing skills in the clinical setting, campus demonstrations, role playing, simulated games, and other strategies may be utilized to teach clinical skills and meet the need for "hands on" involvement.

The use of preceptors may still pose a threat to some faculty. A reluctance to acknowledge the preceptor as being adequately qualified may be a first sign of conflict, regardless of how well the preceptor meets the objective criteria for selection. The feeling that no one is quite good enough for "my" student is common. This may be similar to the dilemma faced by parents who must "let go" of their children and entrust part of their care to others. Evaluating one's own needs and motivations and asking the question, "Whose need am I meeting?" can help to maintain a realistic perspective.

Having accepted the idea of a preceptor, the faculty member may feel a need to exercise a great deal of control in developing the preceptorship. There is a fine line between controlling the quality of the learning experience and controlling each activity in the process. Overcontrol results in frustration by all. The preceptor may feel devalued and unneeded because of a lack of personal and direct involvement in the implementation phase. The faculty may be frustrated because of the resistance encountered. The student, attempting to meet the needs of both and resolve the conflict, may be placed in a middle position between the faculty and preceptor. The priority of learning may thus be sacrificed and replaced by the priority of survival.

The faculty are responsible for determining minimal core objectives of the learning experience and for ensuring a quality experience consistent with those objectives. There must be flexibility in selecting appropriate strategies and methodologies to attain the objectives. The preceptor, student, and available agency resources will help determine the strategies and methodologies. In the event a consistent, standardized approach is essential, the faculty must work with the preceptor to accomplish it.

While the preceptorship is in progress, the faculty member may become critical of activities in the clinical area and feel that the faculty member would have functioned more effectively than the preceptor. This conclusion may be correct; however, the faculty member must approach the situation with a positive attitude and realize that learning occurs in a variety of situations and with many different methodologies, each offering advantages and disadvantages. The faculty task is to maintain the focus on learning outcomes.

Where the faculty perceives education as a mutual, interactive process, with the student assuming the main responsibility for learning, there may be less need to control the situation. The use of a preceptor requires a relatively secure and mature educator. However, for some faculty, the preceptorship process may be too frustrating, and acknowledgment of this fact may be the most effective solution.

**Potential Abuses**

Another concern is to prevent abuse in the preceptorship. Preceptor abuse may be in terms of time or energy demands. The preceptor's prime commitment is to the employing institution; therefore, careful consideration must be given to the time and energy requirements imposed by the preceptorship. Thorough preplanning is essential to delineate the preceptor's roles and responsibilities and to provide a realistic focus for the learning activities. Time requirements should be explicitly stated so that the preceptor is fully cognizant of the demands involved.

Most preceptors and agency administrators perceive the experience as worth their time. They recognize that students make a valuable contribution by providing stimulation to the staff as concerns and questions are posed, new content and skills demonstrated, and resources shared. However, the client or consumer is the one who ultimately benefits from the resulting higher standard of care that may be delivered. Preceptors are usually gratified by being perceived as expert clinicians who offer a reality-based learning experience. It is also rewarding to witness student learning as the students apply theories in their interactions with clients. Finally, recognition by the affiliated university may improve the preceptor's status among the preceptor's peers.

Faculty also may be abused in terms of time demands. During the initial phases of the preceptorship, the student and preceptor may need extra reassurance as they each explore their new roles and try to meet expectations of self and others appropriately. The faculty member should assess this situation and reinforce the strengths and resources of each, but may need to set limits to foster independence and growth.

Care must also be taken to prevent student abuse. Students may be put in the bind of trying to please two masters—each with different expectations. To prevent this, the learning plan must be planned and administered in a consistent, coordinated manner. For their part, the students may try to pit the faculty against the preceptor or assume a helpless, victim role to avoid responsibility. The faculty should work with the student to prevent this from occurring.

**Mutual Trust and Respect**

It may be difficult for the faculty member to accept that another individual may be as competent or more competent in a given clinical area and could be utilized as a vital adjunct to the typical learning experience involving the faculty person, student, and client. Still, the educator cannot be expected to maintain excellent clinical skills in all nursing fields and may come to value the role of the clinician preceptor.

Historically, there has been a gap between nursing service and nursing education, with each faction behaving rather defensively and cautiously toward the other. The traditional educational approach has served to reinforce this separateness. Students were educated and supervised by faculty who frequently sheltered them from the realities of the work world. Ideals were promulgated without considering practicality and feasibility. Students learned to play the game of behaving in the prescribed mode for a grade, yet questioned whether what they were practicing would be workable upon graduation when they joined the "real" world.

Thus, some students may be very critical of the clinical setting to the extent they are concerned about the ideals being implemented. The faculty may assist such students to articulate their concerns and to engage in discussions of how the real and the ideal can mesh together in a relevant, meaningful balance.

The practice of using preceptors to facilitate student learning provides a bridge between nursing education and service. Through joint activities, mutual trust and respect begin to grow and collaboration replaces isolation. Both groups become more aware of their respective contributions as they share the common goal of quality nursing care delivered to clients. In essence, they join the same team and unite their efforts toward goal achievement. Both students and clients benefit greatly from this approach.

The mutual sharing of knowledge and experience is valuable and gratifying. The preceptor may be invited to participate in classroom activities through panel discussions, guest lectures, case conferences, and so on. Faculty may assist the agency by providing consultation, offering inservice education, sharing scarce resources, and so forth. Each may be appointed to advisory councils, serve on joint committees, or have joint appointments. In these ways, maximum effort should be made to bridge the gap and promote collaboration between nursing service and nursing education. Other issues and concerns that may surface can be resolved on the basis of commitments from the faculty person, preceptor, and student.

The faculty should consider various ways to make the preceptorship experience as positive as possible for all involved. These methods should include (1) thorough preplanning to capitalize on the most effective use of preceptor and student time; (2) effective communication with both preceptor and student to provide mutual understanding, continuity, and evaluation; and (3) respect for both as responsible adults.

**REFERENCE**

Wilson, H.S., & Kneisl, C.R. *Psychiatric Nursing.* Menlo Park, Calif.: Addison-Wesley, 1979.

# Chapter 6

# How To Orient a New Preceptor

*Jean M. Haberlin*

The success of the preceptorship depends, to a large degree, on the quality of the preceptor orientation. Orientation is the first step in establishing a trusting, supportive relationship between the program coordinator and the preceptor. Due to the independent nature of the preceptorship, this first step is extremely important. In the initial contact, the coordinator must create an atmosphere that is conducive to open communication and collaboration during all phases of the preceptorship. Orientation also serves the important function of minimizing the anxiety the preceptor may initially feel in undertaking the new experience. By providing a thorough introduction to the program and guidelines for optimizing the experience, for both the preceptor and the student, some of this apprehension will be alleviated, enabling the preceptor to anticipate a positive, meaningful experience with the student.

## GROUP OR INDIVIDUAL ORIENTATION

The orientation of a clinical preceptor may be approached in one of two ways; it may take place in a group situation or on an individual basis. Program needs and time constraints will dictate, to a certain extent, the manner in which the orientation is conducted at a particular time. Group orientation is advantageous in that it provides an opportunity for preceptors to interact with each other and to share their suggestions, experiences, and feelings related to precepting, thus helping to make the orientation a more stimulating and educational experience. The result of this close interaction may be the formation of a "preceptor support group" that can be utilized throughout the preceptorship.

Group orientation also gives the program coordinator the opportunity to observe the social style and interactive patterns of individual preceptors as they relate to other members of the group. This information can be helpful both in choosing a compatible preceptor for a particular student and in assisting the student in resolving any interpersonal problems that may arise during the placement. In addition, if the program is operating under time or travel constraints, group orientation provides an efficient and economical means of accomplishing the orientation of several preceptors.

Individual orientation also has several advantages, one of them being that it allows more flexibility in structure. It can be conducted in a less formal style, thus making it more conducive to spontaneous interaction and providing an opportunity for the preceptor and coordinator to get to know each other well and to develop a close, supportive relationship. Individual orientation may be conducted in the preceptor's clinical setting. This provides an opportunity for the coordinator to become better acquainted with the facility and its personnel.

Ideally, if circumstances allow, the coordinator can combine the benefits of individual and group orientation. The coordinator can visit the health care facility to meet the preceptor and administrative personnel prior to the orientation and then conduct orientation in a small group of six to eight preceptors. This offers the preceptor the advantage of individual contact with the coordinator in addition to the benefits derived from the group orientation.

## FORMAT AND STRUCTURE

The format of the preceptor orientation, whether conducted in a group or individual setting, should include an introduction to program goals; an outline of the organizational structure of the preceptorship; a description of the responsibilities of preceptor, coordinator and student; and information regarding the legalities involved in the preceptor-student relationship. In addition, the orientation should include a discussion of the preceptor's role, expectations, concerns, and questions.

In discussing the goals of the preceptorship, it is important to stress that a preceptorship is intended to be a mutually beneficial experience for both the student and the preceptor. For the student, the preceptorship provides a unique opportunity to develop expertise and confidence in a chosen specialty. At the same time, the preceptorship allows the student to assume the major responsibility for the learning experience. The specific goals and objectives for the preceptorship are determined to a large degree by the student, and the ultimate responsibility for achieving these rests with the student. The student is expected to exercise and develop initiative and assertiveness in fulfilling the objectives through specific, supervised clinical activities.

Preceptorships also serve the important function of alleviating some of the reality shock inherent in the transition from student nurse to graduate nurse. The student is afforded the opportunity to develop independently both the clinical and the interpersonal skills necessary to function at a professional level. Perhaps for the first time in the student's nursing education, the role model is a practicing clinician rather than a nursing instructor. The student is able to observe the preceptor in daily interactions with clients and coworkers and in efforts to integrate the personal and professional aspects of life.

The benefits to the preceptor are perhaps less obvious but no less important. The preceptor has the opportunity to teach an enthusiastic, motivated, and interested student; and this, in itself, can be extremely rewarding to a practitioner whose own enthusiasm may be waning. In this relationship, the opportunities for a mutual exchange of ideas are plentiful. In this way, the student benefits from the preceptor's practical skills and expertise, while the preceptor gains from exposure to the student's new knowledge and perspectives. But, perhaps the most rewarding and satisfying aspect for the preceptor is the knowledge that the student's increase in self-confidence and professionalism is a direct result of the student's relationship with the preceptor.

During orientation, it is important for the program coordinator to outline clearly the structure of the program, from the initial contact through the final evaluation phase. This may be best accomplished by providing an overview that describes and integrates the communications of all participants in chronological sequence, as in Table 6–1.

## INITIAL STEPS

Following the program overview, the coordinator can describe in detail the responsibilities of each participant: preceptor, coordinator, and student. One of the preceptor's initial responsibilities is to meet with the student on the first day of the placement to orient the student, initiate a supportive working relationship, and develop a tentative plan for the preceptorship. The importance of a thorough student orientation cannot be overemphasized. This will help immensely in decreasing the student's level of anxiety to the point where the learning process can begin to take place. One of the unique aspects of a preceptorship is that the student is provided the opportunity to be an active part of the health care team and to begin the socialization process necessary in the transition from student to grad-

**Table 6–1** Preceptorship Program Overview

| Participant | Interaction/Communication |
| --- | --- |
| Coordinator → Student | Introduce and explain preceptorship program |
| Student → Coordinator | Submit application |
| Coordinator → Student's former nursing instructor | Obtain recommendation for student's participation |
| Coordinator ↔ Student | Discuss learning objectives and possible placement sites |
| Coordinator ↔ Agency represent-ative/preceptor | Discuss possible placement |
| Coordinator → Student | Confirm placement |
| Coordinator → Preceptor | Confirm placement |
| Coordinator ↔ Preceptor | Meet/preceptor orientation |
| Student ↔ Preceptor | Telephone contact and/or meet prior to placement |
| Student → Preceptor | Arrival |
| Coordinator ↔ Preceptor | Telephone contact (discuss problems, if any) |
| Coordinator ↔ Student | Telephone contact (discuss problems, if any) |
| Coordinator ↔ Student ↔ Pre-ceptor | Site visit |
| Coordinator ↔ All students cur-rently enrolled in preceptorship course | Seminar |
| Preceptor ↔ Student | Evaluation |
| Coordinator ↔ Student | Evaluation |
| Coordinator ↔ Preceptor/agency representative | Evaluation |

uate. This cannot occur, however, until the student is familiar and comfortable with the surroundings and feels accepted. Prior to placement, staff members should be made aware of the student's role and objectives so that they can assist the preceptor in including the student as part of the health care team and in identifying valuable learning experiences.

During the initial meeting, it is crucial that the student and preceptor discuss each other's expectations for the learning experience and clarify the student's role within the agency. It is appropriate at this point for the preceptor to state explicitly expectations regarding student attendance, the level of participation the student can expect, and guidelines for student-patient interaction. The preceptor also needs to know the student's level of experience, self-confidence, and personal background, as well as the student's professional interests, concerns, and limitations. The one-to-one learning relationship between student and preceptor is an intense and personal one. The initial discussion provides the opportunity to develop a trusting relationship, one that allows the student to acknowledge both accomplishments and mistakes in a supportive atmosphere.

Early in the placement, the preceptor and student should carefully review the learning objectives and discuss ways in which each can be fulfilled. The preceptor can then develop, with the student, a plan that will ensure adequate clinical supervision and fulfillment of learning objectives. It may be necessary to modify, add, or delete objectives. At this time, it may also be appropriate to discuss or plan learning experiences outside the placement facility if the student's objectives seem to indicate that this may be necessary or desirable. After a general plan for the student's time has been determined, it is advisable to develop a tentative calendar indicating the days and times the student plans to spend in the facility so that the staff is aware of the schedule. This helps to ensure that the preceptor will be available to supervise the student. There of course may be times when the preceptor is unavailable. In these instances, the preceptor may delegate the responsibility to another staff member of comparable expertise or, if this is not feasible, request that the student alter the schedule. If the student works with a substitute preceptor, it is essential that all involved parties be agreeable to the arrangement. Those who must be informed include the student, the substitute preceptor, the supervisor, and/or the director of nurses.

## REQUIREMENTS AND EVALUATION

It is the responsibility of the preceptor to make appropriate daily clinical assignments based on a realistic assessment of the student's theoretical knowledge and clinical expertise. Since the duration of the preceptorship is relatively short, it is important that the preceptor be made fully aware of the student's clinical strengths and weaknesses as soon as possible. There are various methods that can be used to obtain this information, but perhaps the most useful is a written skills list completed by the student prior to, or on, the first day of the placement. By reviewing this list, the preceptor can foresee the amount of supervision the student is likely to require and can make clinical assignments that will be both realistic and challenging. The use of a skills list helps to ensure that the student will receive appropriate supervision and, at the same time, will direct efforts toward the acquisition of new knowledge and skills.

The preceptor will also be required to provide one or more written student evaluations during the preceptorship. These evaluations are designed to assess not only the student's ability to meet the objectives, but also the student's attitude and the manner in which the student demonstrates a professional commitment to patients, staff, preceptor, and agency. These evaluations are also valuable for the preceptor in that they provide a means of determining the adequacy of the preceptor's teaching methods. The preceptor and the student should review these written evaluations together to compare their perceptions about the student's performance and to discuss and clarify any discrepancies. (See Chapter 21 for a detailed discussion of evaluation procedures in preceptorship programs.)

In addition to the required periodic evaluations, the preceptor should be encouraged to meet with the student on a daily basis to provide ongoing evaluation and answer questions pertaining to the student's clinical performance. This is especially critical in the initial stages of the preceptorship when the student is feeling anxious and insecure. These meetings can become more brief and concise as the preceptorship progresses and the student develops confidence. In addition to the exchange of feedback specific to daily clinical activities, weekly conferences may be held for the purpose of assessing the progress being made on objectives, planning clinical activities, and managing any problems that may arise.

At this point in the orientation, the preceptor may be feeling overwhelmed by the investment of time and energy that seems to be necessary. It is important for the coordinator to acknowledge this feeling and the fact that both preceptor and student may experience some initial frustrations until they establish a pattern of activities and interactions. Eventually, however, the relationship will become more reciprocal; and the student, within the limits of the established objectives, can begin to assume more responsibility and provide increased assistance to the preceptor.

During the orientation, the program coordinator will want to discuss the coordinator's role in the placement, including the coordinator's availability and planned interaction with the student and preceptor during the placement. One of the coordinator's first responsibilities is to ensure that the students selected have met the criteria established by the preceptorship program. These criteria will, of course, vary depending on the particular program; still the coordinator should be aware of each student's level of academic and clinical preparation.

## INDIVIDUAL STUDENT NEEDS AND RESPONSIBILITIES

After the student has been screened and accepted for participation in the preceptorship, the coordinator will need to discuss with the preceptor the specific student assigned to the preceptor. If the preceptor orientation is individual, this can be done in conjunction with the orientation session. However, if the orientation is conducted in a group setting, the coordinator will need to arrange a time to do this. Included in this discussion should be information related to the student's need for supervision, level of maturity, clinical strengths and weaknesses, communication and social skills, past nursing experience, and career goals. Also at this time, the program coordinator should provide the preceptor with a general description of the curriculum of the participating nursing school, the course the student is currently enrolled in, and the educational objectives established for the preceptorship. The student may have academic requirements, in addition to clinical assignments, that will have to be fulfilled during the preceptorship; for example, the student may be required to maintain a daily journal, write a paper related to some aspect of the learning experience, and so on. It is important that the preceptor be made aware of these requirements and understand their purpose and relevance.

Prior to placement, the program coordinator is also responsible for reviewing, with the preceptor, each student's objectives. Each objective should be considered for its relevance and feasibility within the specific health care agency. Depending on the resources available within the agency, some objectives may need to be modified or deleted. Others may not be feasible within the primary placement facility but could be fulfilled in other nearby health care facilities. Suggestions can be generated between the coordinator and preceptor as to facilities that may fulfill some of the objectives and provide an additional learning experience. For example, a student may be placed in a small, acute care hospital but may also wish to fulfill some objectives related to public health. This can be accomplished through a cooperative arrangement between the placement agency representative and/or program coordinator and the public health department.

During the preceptor orientation, the coordinator will need to discuss the plan for maintaining oral and/or written communication with the preceptor and the student. This may be accomplished through a variety of means. The coordinator may meet individually with the student and preceptor at various times in addition to meeting with both of them periodically. The frequency and content of these meetings will vary according to the design of the preceptorship program. The preceptor should be given specific information regarding the frequency of such conferences, the type of preparation the preceptor is responsible for, estimated length of the meetings, and so on. The coordinator may also request and/or initiate telephone calls or letters as a means of assessing each student's progress. In this case, it is important that the coordinator provide the preceptor with the details regarding the telephone calls or letters.

The coordinator will want to stress the fact that the coordinator is available by phone to provide ongoing assistance in accomplishing learning objectives and managing any communication problems that may arise. It is extremely reassuring to the preceptor to know that the coordinator will in most instances be available by phone to listen and assist in any situation, even those that the preceptor may consider "insignificant." The preceptor can also be assured that, if problems arise during the placement that cannot be satisfactorily resolved, the program coordinator will assume the responsibility for withdrawing the student, if that becomes necessary.

On the student's part, an ability and willingness to exercise a high degree of initiative and assertiveness will be the major determinant in the outcome of the learning experience. Prior to the placement, the student will be responsible for developing behavioral objectives as the basis for clinical activities. The objectives may be written entirely by the student, or they may be a collaborative effort between the student and program coordinator. In either case, the student will often find it necessary to modify or rewrite the objectives as the placement proceeds. This is to be expected, and in fact encouraged, if doing so will allow the student to take advantage of a larger variety of quality clinical experiences.

The student has the ultimate responsibility for ensuring that the clinical objectives are met. Although the preceptor assists in developing the plan and facilitating its implementation, the student must be committed to carrying out the plan.

Most importantly, during all phases of the placement, the student must take responsibility for communicating effectively with the preceptor, agency staff, and program coordinator regarding clinical activities, learning objectives, and any problems that may arise. This, as noted earlier, specifically involves meeting daily with the preceptor, maintaining telephone and/or written communication with the coordinator, meeting with the coordinator as required, and participating in the evaluation process.

## LEGAL AND POLICY ASPECTS

At some point during the orientation, the legal aspects of the preceptorship should be addressed by the coordinator. Unfortunately, at the present time, there are very few specific, written legal guidelines governing the preceptor-student relationship. (Chapter 18, however, outlines some of the basic legal considerations that the preceptor should be aware of.)

In addition, each facility will have specific policies and regulations applicable to students. These may be formal, written policies, or they may be flexible and informal policies. In either case, the preceptor will need to discuss the legal aspect of the preceptorship with the agency administrator and become familiar with the relevant policies. Some preceptors may work with students who are licensed, practicing nurses returning to college to obtain a baccalaureate degree. However, it is important to stress that even the most competent, experienced nurse is still operating as a "student" while in the facility. Thus, though the supervision necessary for this type of student may be minimal, the preceptor must always remain aware of the fact that the preceptor is still, in part, legally responsible for the student's actions.

## THE PRECEPTOR'S TEACHING ROLE

During orientation, the program coordinator may wish to discuss briefly the teaching role as it applies to precepting. The preceptor's ability to create and maintain an atmosphere that allows and encourages independent, self-directed learning is crucial to the success of the preceptorship. The preceptor must feel comfortable in the role and confident as a teacher. In an effort to make the presentation of teaching techniques more systematic, the coordinator may wish to consider separately four aspects of the teaching role. The questions included in the following discussion of these aspects provide a means of translating teaching theory into specific preceptor behavior that can be objectively measured by both the student and preceptor (Simon, 1976).

The four teaching aspects or roles are, for purposes of discussion, examined separately. In reality, it is not possible to make clear distinctions between them. Ideally, the preceptor will be adept at each, emphasizing one or more as circumstances dictate.

### The Preceptor As Role Model

Role modeling is an extremely effective mode of teaching, yet it is one that the preceptor cannot "prepare for." The student learns by observing, analyzing, and questioning the preceptor's style of practice, interactions with clients and colleagues, and responses to a multitude of personal and professional demands. As a role model, the preceptor has the responsibility of maintaining a level of self-awareness that allows the preceptor to reflect on behavior, motives, and feelings with the student. This provides the student with the rationale underlying the preceptor's observable actions and decisions. In the self-questioning the preceptor may ask:

- How many times did you meet with the student? Did you allow the student an exchange of feedback?
- Did you feel there was open communication and trust between you and the student?
- Did you offer support to the student? How?

**The Preceptor As Designer of Instruction**

For the preceptor, acting as a designer of instruction may be the most unfamiliar teaching role. This role emphasizes the planning phase of the instructional process and formalizes the function of structuring the teaching and learning experience. Each behavioral objective should be analyzed by the preceptor and student in an effort to determine the specific clinical activities that will lead to the fulfillment of the objectives. These clinical activities will then constitute the plan to be implemented and eventually evaluated. In this role, the following questions should be asked:

- Did you and the student take the opportunity to discuss each other's expectations for the learning experience?
- Did you give the student an orientation?
- Did you introduce the student to the staff?
- Was the student accepted, made to feel a part of the staff?
- Did you analyze, *with* the student, the meaning of the student's objectives?
- Were you able to provide or suggest useful and interesting experiences to meet the student's objectives?
- Did you plan the educational experiences with the student?
- Was there optimum use of the student's time?
- Based on the agreed-upon objectives and the plan for implementing the instruction, did both you and the student participate in an ongoing evaluation of the student's progress?

**The Preceptor As Resource Person**

The student should be encouraged to use the most appropriate resource available, which, in many cases, will *not* be the preceptor. Often, due to the availability of the preceptor, students do not take advantage of other resources. The preceptor should be used as a resource only when it is determined that the preceptor is the most appropriate source of instruction in a particular knowledge or skill area. The relevant questions here are:

- Were you willing to share your expertise?
- Did you take the time to demonstrate procedures, and so on, when appropriate?

- Were you able to assist the student in finding other resources when appropriate?
- Were the demonstrations and explanations clear to the student? How did you know?

**The Preceptor As Supervisor**

The primary goal of clinical supervision is to increase the student's professional autonomy. The preceptor facilitates this process by creating conditions that encourage the student to take the initiative in examining and modifying the student's behavior or knowledge. Clinical supervision demands a relatively passive role for the preceptor and an active role for the student. The relevant questions in this role are:

- Did you feel you provided appropriate supervision? Academic? Clinical?
- Did you have weekly conferences with the student?
- Did you share your viewpoint with the student, rather than impose it?
- Did you encourage self-initiation, individuality, self-expression and self-evaluation?

**CONCLUSION**

At the conclusion of the orientation, it is extremely important that the preceptor be encouraged to discuss any questions or concerns and, in general, to share expectations regarding the experience. This will help immensely in clarifying the material presented and in alleviating any apprehension the preceptor may be experiencing. Thus, the preceptor will leave the orientation having gained the confidence and knowledge necessary to implement the preceptorship program successfully.

**REFERENCE**

Simon, M.P.A. *A role guide and resource book for clinical preceptors* (U.S. DHEW, Publication Number [HRA] 77–14). Washington, D.C.: U.S. Government Printing Office, 1976.

# Chapter 7

# How To Establish Rapport with an Off-Campus Person

*Phyllis Schubert*

## THE PROBLEM

Why is it important for nurse educators to build relationships in the community? The reason is found in the charge of higher education in nursing that nurses be prepared with the requisite knowledge and skills to meet the nursing needs of society (Heidgerken, 1965).

As nursing responds to an everchanging and dynamic world, nursing must be constantly redefined. It must be responsive to the shifts in philosophy evidenced by legislative acts, court decisions, and funds provided for research and education as well as to the events that make demands on nurses, such as physical catastrophes and social developments. These constant changes require an ongoing dialogue between those in the nursing profession and the various components of the community.

It is imperative that nurse educators build strong working relationships with nurses outside the educational institution, with persons in other disciplines, and with consumers of different life styles and belief systems. Such relationships provide the media for meaningful dialogue toward change and redefinition.

On the other hand, nursing education must be responsible not only to the community and society but also to the student who seeks to serve society through the role of nursing. The student is guided through a process that prepares the student for a profession that is everchanging in response to a society in which change occurs at an everincreasing pace. Graduates who will be working with rapid change must be prepared not only to expect, but more importantly, to shape changes, to be flexible and skilled in problem solving. Creativity in the formation of alternative solutions is a highly desired trait in leaders of health care systems.

The development of the potential in the individual nursing student is another aspect of educational responsibility. Since the field of nursing is increasingly complex and diverse, it requires that educators encourage diverse interests, abilities, and talents in students. Nurses and other health professionals in varied settings can join the educational team in preparing the student for roles suited to the uniqueness of the individual learner. Different nursing styles are necessary, appropriate to different settings and populations. The tasks are myriad, involving technical skills, health education, counseling, management, and research. Physical, psychological, cultural, and spiritual assessments must be provided for individuals, families, populations, communities, and societies. The resulting great diversity in nursing requires creativity, flexibility, and respect for people of various value systems.

Nurses provide services in institutions, agencies, homes, and other community settings. Community settings can range from a car or a meadow to an old abandoned school house. Nurses in rural settings find themselves repairing electric cords and plumbing, or wishing there was electricity and plumbing. They may find themselves sitting on the back step with a frightened woman, exploring the possibilities for getting a sick husband to a physician 50 miles away. Thus, every aspect of the nurse's being, especially ingenuity, is called upon as the nurse is challenged to care for people in the health-illness experiences of their lives.

Some nurses find this kind of demand on their resources highly satisfying and rewarding. Others find it dull and parochial and prefer the fast pace of the acute care hospital. In any case, as nurses develop and serve in their various potentialities, the nursing needs of a complex and diverse society are met.

## COLLABORATION BETWEEN NURSING EDUCATION AND THE COMMUNITY

Nurses can be educated most effectively through the combined effort of educators and community people, including nurses in clinical settings, health professionals, and consumers. It is of course very desirable that nursing educators be involved in nursing service, but that situation is difficult to attain. Some educators have joint appointments in clinical roles, some are involved in research projects with community agencies, and others are involved in nursing service only during the summer months.

Another way to establish more communication between the community and nursing educators is by establishing liaison with nurses working in a broad variety of clinical settings. These nurses, serving as preceptors, can provide supervision and guidance for individual students as they are involved in learning experiences suited to their unique interests and talents.

The placement of students in acute care hospitals and in public health departments under the supervision of nursing faculty is an accepted practice in nursing education. Preceptorships provide exposure of the students to a wide selection of nursing experiences. The selected setting can provide an environment in which the student can meet personal learning objectives. Generally, the preceptor is a highly qualified nurse or physician who serves as a role model, resource person, consultant, and supervisor for the student.

Students can be involved, then, in various settings and can share their experiences in seminars with classmates and instructors. The student, the classmates, the department of nursing, the agency of placement, the preceptor and the faculty all benefit from the combined effort. Such collaboration with the community also helps to lessen the "reality shock" for new graduates. Practitioners and clinicians can keep abreast of current theory, practices and trends in education. The communication involved promotes a trusting relationship between the educational institution and the community. As a result, nursing education becomes more responsive to society and is better able to meet societal needs.

Because care for the whole person requires a multidisciplinary approach, students must be prepared to work interdependently with persons of various professions. Cooperation and dialogue between persons of various professions are necessary. The placement of advanced students in health agency settings with preceptors puts them in a position to take part in the dialogue. They must define their roles in relation to that of the other staff members while meeting their own learning objectives. When the students do this successfully—and most of them do—they experience a team effort and, as a team member, boost their own self-confidence and self-esteem.

The role of the nurse overlaps with that of many health professionals, such as physicians, psychologists, social workers, health educators, physical therapists, nutritionists, physician assistants, psychiatric technicians, and environmental health workers. The overlap creates vague boundaries and sensitive areas that demand skills in interpersonal relationships and communication. Because nurses serve as advocates for clients in a mass of entangled relationships within the health care system, a lack of communication and coordination can create problems for clients.

Both nursing practice and nursing education need more communication with consumers and consumer groups. Consumers are becoming more vocal and more forceful in asking for services that are relevant to their needs and consonant with their belief systems. Consumers give valuable feedback and information when professionals are brave enough to listen. Educators must thus extend themselves into the community and really listen. The anger one hears is sometimes frightening to health care providers. But it is always challenging! By listening with care and respect we can learn what must be done to make health care services more helpful to consumers. Through dialogue, trust can be created, and therapeutic relationships can be established.

## ATTITUDES THAT HELP TO CREATE RAPPORT

What are some of the attitudes of the nurse educator that can foster positive working relationships with off-campus persons? The following approaches to off-campus people, applicable to nursing service personnel, other health professionals, and consumers of various life styles, are examples of attitudes based on honesty and truth:

- *Your skills and knowledge are valuable to the school of nursing and our students.* Your agency, setting, and staff have been selected because of their uniqueness in what they have to offer a student or group of students. Your skills, knowledge base, experience, and philosophy are respected by us. We can learn from what you have to offer.
- We are interested in your program, your experiences, and beliefs concerning the health care of clients, families, and community groups. *Would you be interested in sharing your experiences with the department of nursing?* (Nurses and their support staffs develop provider systems based upon their values, and they appreciate the opportunity to share their programs with students and faculty. They realize that exposure to outside ideas and research leads to improvement in services and education. Research findings can be shared on a personal level that is meaningful and exciting to everyone concerned. The agencies also get an opportunity to recruit nurses for themselves or for other agencies with similar programs.)
- We have something we believe is valuable to you and your agency. *We want to share it with you.* We can share through discussion, through inservice and continuing education programs, and through research projects and exchange of materials. Your ideas will be considered through ongoing curriculum evaluation and change in our program. We will search for ways to have more community input in curriculum planning. Our work together will result in a relationship between you and our educational institution that will enhance growth—yours, ours, and the students'.
- *We recognize your time is valuable.* Let us keep our meetings short and adhere closely to time schedules. We have a goal to be organized, concise, and clear in our communications. There must be time, however, for any concerns or issues you wish to discuss.

- Your energy is also valuable. We will work toward maximum efficiency of resources for a quality student experience. *Let us keep it simple while striving to be as effective as possible.* Paperwork will be kept to a minimum.

In addition to the above attitudes, there are others that can promote rapport between nursing instructors and preceptors:

- *You have been selected as a preceptor because of your abilities that set you apart as a role model in your area of nursing.* You are recognized for your ability and interest in teaching. Your position provides an opportunity to serve as a resource person and leader in an area of interest to students.
- *We respect you and trust you to carry through with our agreement.* We will work together and notify each other of any concerns regarding the student's learning experience.
- *We are interested in your contribution* toward the evaluation of our program and in your suggestions for improvement.
- *We are a team.* Together we can provide an environment for the student to prepare for a successful future in nursing.
- We will make mistakes. We cannot take risks and never make mistakes. We cannot avoid risk taking and also provide a dynamic and relevant education in nursing. *However, we do promise to learn from our mistakes.* We will strive to keep them infrequent and minimal.

With some adaptation, these statements can also apply to therapeutic attitudes of nurses and nurse educators toward consumers:

- We encourage and support you as you search for ways to improve your health. We can serve as resources for you and provide counsel, information, and alternatives to aid you in finding appropriate solutions in your lives. *But we respect your right to make decisions for your own health care.*
- *We are vitally interested in you as whole persons.* Your beliefs, feelings, and life styles must be considered in the formation of a plan to increase your health and well-being.
- *Your time, energy, and money* are all important. We respect your time and energy, so we will not keep you waiting. We will keep the costs as low as possible while providing the agreed-upon services. (Clients wait long hours in our institutions for services, and then we wonder why they do not return for follow-up care. Waiting is a humiliating

experience and should be minimized in order to encourage feelings of self-worth and self-respect. The cost of health care is also discouraging to clients. Every effort should be made to eliminate unnecessary cost and to involve the client in cost decisions. Clients are discouraged by high costs, even when they are covered by a third party payer, and they are devastated when there is no financial coverage for medical bills.)

Finally, there are specific attitudes that can foster therapeutic environments with peoples of different cultural beliefs and practices regarding health and illness:

- *We are here to serve your health needs as you have identified them.* Our relationship with you must be one of mutual respect and trust. Building trust will take time, but we are willing to take the necessary time to develop that trust.

- *We want to improve health care services to your people.* (People often suffer indignities and are subjected to frightening and humiliating experiences when they are hospitalized or when they go to clinics. When they feel we care for them and want to make their experience more helpful, they will participate in dialogue.)

- *We would like to learn from you.* Would you teach us about your cultural beliefs so that we can understand and provide care within your belief framework? We recognize that our system does not have all the answers for people experiencing pain and distress in their lives. There is much we can learn from other cultural systems of health care. Most systems outside Western medicine focus on the whole person rather than a single diseased part, and we are learning that our way is not necessarily always the best. A synthesis of folk practice and professional medicine may be the best solution for many problems (Leininger, 1978). One way you can help us to learn is by accepting our students into your health care systems and helping us to educate them in transcultural nursing practices.

- *We need guidance by your people as to what kind of services are needed by them.* Without such guidance, we may assume that health education is not important to that group and that that is the way they want it. On the other hand, the group's concerns and identified needs may not be what a health professional would expect.

## RELATIONSHIP PROBLEMS

There are some problem areas in educator-preceptor understanding that require increased attention to communication patterns and skills. Communication involves listening and hearing, talking, and being heard. Differences in communication may arise when the educator has more formal education in nursing than the preceptor and may also have a broader perspective of the field of nursing, its issues and trends. On the other hand, the preceptor is often more highly skilled in a specific area of nursing, focused on one set of services to an identified population in a particular setting. Nurses often have extraordinary expertise in a health care setting but may not see nursing care within the broader system of family, community, and society. They may not perceive that legislation, grant writing, community assessment, health planning, and management skills have anything to do with nursing or hands-on patient care. In such a situation, patience, understanding, and a desire to understand and to learn are required on both sides.

Another difference in perspective may be in time orientation. The practitioner is oriented to the present and near future, while the educator is focused more on the student being prepared for future practice. The instructor's emphasis is on the nursing student as a leader in health care planning and delivery over a future period of 30 to 40 years. The preceptor will often be concerned with much shorter time frames (unless the preceptor is involved in long-range state, federal, or international program planning).

There are biases about which kind of nursing is "real nursing." Practitioners may feel that students should receive more education in their own chosen area. Some demand more medical-surgical training for students, while others may insist on more community health or rural nursing. Such disputes can be interesting, but the fact is that all areas of nursing are necessary. Let us not forget that the basic issue is to give total care to whole people as they live the health-illness experience.

As noted earlier, nurse educators and other health professionals in the community may have relationship problems that seem to arise predominantly from questions regarding boundaries between disciplines. This often involves a lack of understanding of work roles. In such situations, education and staff meetings to work through questions regarding job descriptions and definitions are necessary.

Students who become involved in such conflicts require a broadminded, flexible, and culturally experienced instructor to provide guidance. The achievement of a healthy perspective toward interdisciplinary cooperation and role definition in the particular setting is a major task.

Probably the most serious issues for nursing education and practice arise from disenchantment among consumers regarding the health care system and its workers. An angry public will seek revenge through noncompliance and malpractice suits. Families are seeking help from unqualified persons in an attempt to provide hospitals and other institutions of medicine. A more healthy approach, which some lay persons are taking, is to educate themselves in medical self-care. This is a new trend among a significant minority in this society.

Educated consumers are demanding that they be consulted and involved in planning for their own care. They feel they are in charge of their own health and should make the decisions regarding care and treatment. They also want information regarding alternatives and often ask for advice. Respect requires acknowledgment of the right of the consumer to make choices, and also to make mistakes and to learn from those mistakes.

Consumers are asking that their beliefs and value systems be considered when a plan for care is developed and instituted. One aspect of cultural values that is often neglected in the nursing care of hospitalized patients concerns the family. In many societies, the individual is recognized basically as a family member. All decisions are made by the family because the family unit is what is important. The individual is seen only in perspective of service to the family. In our society, individual rights are highly valued. Family and group rights do not carry as high a value in our society as they do in other cultures. However, health professions have tended to disregard family care for all cultures and have angered even the American middle-class from which most health professionals come.

Cultural differences imply differences in value systems. These values often conflict with those of professional medicine. Resolution of conflict requires interaction among individuals and groups, with the intent to learn from each other.

Health professionals need to be teachers and resource people to provide information regarding alternatives. Information should be given with counseling for clarification of values, support, and unconditional regard for the client and family/friends; this ensures that the people and their needs are served rather than our own.

## CONCLUSION

Nurse educators recognize the need to be involved with more aspects of nursing service, with other health professions in various settings, and with consumers at different levels of development and with different cultural beliefs.

One way of increasing contact is to assign advanced nursing students to health agency settings where they can achieve individual learning objectives for their chosen area of nursing. These students learn under the guidance and supervision of a preceptor, a nurse, or, in some circumstances, a physician. The preceptor is selected to be a role model, resource person, and supervisor.

The relationship between instructor and preceptor is important because they share a common goal of educating the student. Trust and respect for each other provide  the basis for a positive experience by the student, preceptor, and instructor.

In most settings, a multidisciplinary approach to health care is essential. Healthy relationships among the staff require much communication and skill in interpersonal relationships. Students learn and grow in many ways while working with multidisciplinary teams. Their interpersonal relationship skills increase, and their self-esteem and confidence grow as they experience the satisfaction of working with a team in providing care to clients.

Dialogue between consumers and nurse educators improves the quality of care and promotes trust, respect, and understanding. The attitudes of the nurse educator greatly determine the quality of experience for the persons involved.

Problems will of course be encountered in the relationships between educators, preceptors, other health professionals, and consumers. It is important to develop attitudes that accept the inevitability of such problems and generate a willingness to work them out and to learn from the experience.

---

**REFERENCES**

Heidgerken, L. *Teaching and learning in schools of nursing* (3rd ed.). Philadelphia: J.B. Lippincott Co., 1965.

Leininger, M. *Transcultural nursing: Concepts, theories and practices.* New York: John Wiley & Sons, 1978.

# Chapter 8

# How To Be Comfortable with Students Doing Clinical Work with a Preceptor

*Virginia Young Meyer*

Preceptorship study is a clearly defined course of study to meet individual needs and match the student's interests while identified professional goals are being achieved. It is the faculty member's responsibility to ensure that the clinical learning experience is meaningful and that it fulfills the goals and objectives of the preceptorship course of study. In the traditional clinical experience, the clinical professor is the role model (the observer) who is present in the clinical setting. When preceptors are used to teach clinical nursing, that ongoing personal supervision of the student's clinical practice ceases. The faculty person now assumes a new role, that of facilitating the total preceptorship experience by planning, teaching, counseling, consulting, group leading, and evaluation. In assuming these various roles, the faculty member is aware of the range of the student's clinical experiences. The professor and the student work together to ensure that the student's individualized goals coincide with the preceptorship course goals and objectives. "The preceptorship may include carrying out an investigation, mastering a skill or set of skills, attacking a set of problems, creating a piece of work or otherwise dealing with a specific body of subject matter" (Freed & Landis, 1981, p. 14).

## JOINT PLANNING

Joint cooperation and planning by the student, preceptor, and professor determine student clinical activities and learning experiences. Prior to planning with the student and preceptor, the faculty member needs a thorough understanding of the preceptor's role. A preceptor is a highly qualified professional with a specific expertise. This is the person in the clinical setting with whom the student will work most closely. The preceptor teaches the student in a variety of ways—by guiding the student's inquiry and study, serving as a role model, and supervising the student's clinical field work.

71

The evaluation methods and tools selected by the student and approved by the professor provide a means of evaluating the student's clinical experience. The specificity and appropriateness of these tools, as well as student-faculty conferences and preceptor site visits, establish a means by which the professor may assess the student's clinical experience. It is through this mechanism that the professor maintains control over the quality of the clinical experience, even when the students are doing clinical work that is guided by another person.

## CONTACTS AND COMMUNICATION

There are a number of ways in which the faculty member can enhance knowledge of the student's clinical experiences. Open, freely exchanged communications between student, preceptor, and professor are essential. Site visits at the beginning and end of the preceptorship course of study help to establish a trusting relationship. Site visits also allow the professor to become acquainted with agency staff and administrative policies. In addition, the faculty member can become familiar with the physical setting and overall environment in which the student's preceptorship study will be conducted. Additional visits may be made as appropriate. Student conferences with the faculty person on a regular basis ensure both the instructor and the student opportunities to stay informed of clinical developments. For example, Bird (1981) reports a case where a student commented that her faculty advisor "always displayed enthusiasm and interest in the preceptorship study area. She created a comfortable and safe atmosphere, which enabled me to freely ask questions and to share experiences encountered in the clinical area."

Written work in the form of clinical journals, time logs, case studies, term papers, and verbal reports by the student make it possible for the professor to assess the student's progress. These tools provide the professor with a means to evaluate the ability of the student to report and describe the student's activities, to transfer and apply current and previous knowledge and skills to the clinical setting, and to synthesize, analyze, and solve problems.

## SELECTION OF THE PRECEPTOR

Another factor that will assist the professor to feel comfortable with students doing clinical work under a preceptor's supervision is knowledge of the preceptor's qualifications. If the faculty advisor is convinced and assured of the preceptor's clinical expertise, the advisor may also feel that the clinical skills and knowledge that the student will be observing are also at an exemplary level.

The preceptor is an expert in the field of the selected practice. The preceptor's expertise may be determined by the agency and by peers in the profession or it may be determined by the academic institution. Thus, the preceptor has been identified as a professional who is qualified to assist the student in securing a meaningful educational experience. The preceptor may be a nurse with either a bachelor's or a master's degree. If the preceptor does not have a degree, the faculty advisor may look to other measures of competence and excellence. The preceptor may be a nurse who has many years of experience in the area of practice. (We recommend a minimum of three to five years in practice.) Or the preceptor may have completed a specialized training program or hold a specialty certification (e.g., family nurse practitioner) from a professional organization.

Occasionally a student may want to have a preceptor who is not a nurse. The nonnurse may in fact be the person best prepared to provide the student with a meaningful educational experience. For example, if a student wants to work with clients who have orthopedic conditions, a physical therapist might be selected as a preceptor. Nonhealth professionals may also be suitable preceptors. One student who was interested in the spiritual assessment of hospitalized preoperative and postoperative patients chose to work with a minister in the hospital's pastoral care unit. Another student wanted to blend a nursing skill with musical talents and planned to use a personal musical repertoire during preceptorship study. This student used the music as a means of relaxation and self-expression and as a meaningful vehicle for doing grief work while working with dependent elderly confined to a convalescent hospital. The preceptor the student chose was a music therapist. Even when the preceptor is a professional in a field outside of nursing, the professional's education and experience may be used as criteria to establish competence, thereby providing the necessary expertise for preceptorship study in areas closely related to nursing.

## ROLE MODELING

Another factor that has tremendous influence on the student in preceptorship study is the role model offered by the faculty advisor. Although the professor may feel as if the professor's job of being a role model has been completely relinquished or delegated to the clinical preceptor, many aspects of role modeling still are borne by the academic professor. During site visits, the student will observe the professor as both academician and expert in the clinical area in which the student is doing the practicum. This is a valid observation, since the faculty member is usually an expert in the clinical specialty selected by the student with whom the faculty member works.

The faculty advisor's enthusiasm, interest, and commitment also influence the student's motivation, energy level, and demonstrated competence in the clinical area. Thus, in an example cited by McWhinnie (1981):

> one student, in an evaluation of her faculty advisor noted, "I have found that she has an incredible wealth of knowledge that she is willing (and eager) to share with others. She frequently refers students to other valuable resource persons as well. Although I found this semester of preceptorship study to be very time consuming and difficult, it was one of my most pleasurable clinical experiences and I feel that my faculty advisor was certainly responsible for a large part of the experience.  (p. 2)

Feedback, constructive criticism, and validation of progress toward preceptorship goals and objectives are other powerful means by which the professor influences the student's progress.

## SITE VISITS AND CONFERENCES

The initial site visit is of utmost importance. During this visit, the faculty member, preceptor, and student review the role of each person in the preceptorship study; here beginning rapport should be established. This is an opportunity to clarify expectations and to answer the preceptor's questions about the preceptor role. Upon entering the clinical preceptor role for the first time, the new preceptor may feel inadequately prepared or a lack of the expertise needed to serve as a role model. The initial site visit provides the faculty member with the occasion to assure the first-time preceptor that the preceptor's expertise *is* adequate.

A new preceptor's uneasiness may disappear upon learning that the professor is responsible for the final comprehensive evaluation of the student. Some preceptors may feel responsible for the student's learning all the course work too. They may be unaware that the professor is the person responsible for assessing the student's overall progress and assigning the student's grade. The student's competency in preceptorship study will also be determined by the faculty member. That evaluation will include the preceptor's input and clinical evaluation of the student's level of functioning in the clinical practicum, but it will also be based on the student's other written and verbal work.

Thus it is desirable for the student, preceptor, and faculty advisor to meet for an initial conference at the clinical site. It is also valuable for the faculty advisor to meet with the preceptor prior to or after the conference with the student. This meeting may promote a peer relationship between faculty member and preceptor. It creates an opportunity for an exchange of current information in the specialty field, a sharing of professional philosophies, and a discussion of timely issues. It can provide an occasion for a discussion of proposed action should a change in the agency, clients, or situation prove to be an obstacle to the student participating in a particular learning activity or a certain clinical experience. The mutual trust, respect, and professional collegiality resulting from the preceptor-professor conference may also provide the added rapport that allows a preceptor to contact and clarify an issue with the faculty member before it becomes a problem. An advantage from the professor's point of view is that, the better the rapport with the preceptor, the more comfortable the faculty member will be when that faculty member's students are doing clinical work under another person's guidance.

It is a good rule of thumb to check with the first-time preceptor at midterm. A telephone call may supply what is necessary to reclarify roles or provide a substitute for activities that may be difficult to provide for the student. This will reassure the preceptor of the professor's continued interest and involvement. Simultaneously it will reestablish the faculty member's sense of being aware of the progress of the student at midterm.

The final visit is the occasion for thanking the preceptor for taking the time and energy to offer a meaningful clinical experience to the student. Written preceptor evaluative remarks can be clarified, with the preceptor having the chance to share any additional comments. This visit provides the time for evaluating the clinical learning experience. Excellent activities can be recognized, and improvements in the learning experience can be explored. Finally, the faculty member can use this visit to commend the preceptor for the preceptor's professional contribution.

Site visits establish a set for the faculty member and provide first-hand knowledge of the clinical environment. Conferences between the professor and student furnish time for up-to-date communication about the clinical experience. The student can review the progress made and ask questions. Activities can be revised or eliminated and others substituted. A current time frame can be established. Usually the first few weeks of the preceptorship study require more one-on-one time to work out arrangements, so weekly conferences with the student may be necessary. As a positive working relationship is established, biweekly conferences often suffice.

## EVALUATION

Since the faculty member is not present in the clinical setting, it is necessary to depend on evaluative tools and methods to keep advised of the student's clinical experience. Oral conferences and reports are sources of firsthand information. Written work supplies additional data.

The clinical log of activities documents dates, times, and major activities performed by the student. The log can either be a separate document or be maintained in conjunction with a clinical journal. The clinical journal is a record that includes daily observations, a record of events, and how the student felt about these events. In this way, documentation of experiences is maintained, and the student has the chance to share both positive and negative thoughts and feelings.

A few sample entries from the journal of a school nursing preceptorship student are presented in Exhibit 8–1. The student describes activities and plans with respect to an adolescent parent program sponsored by a large high school district. The entries show how well informed a professor can be after reviewing a clinical journal.

Exhibit 8–1 demonstrates how the clinical journal provides a record of student activities. Positive and negative feelings about the clinical experience are shared in the excerpts in Exhibit 8–2 from another student's journal as the student moved through a semester preceptorship course of study.

The clinical journal also provides a means for the student to request special information or advice from the student's professor. For example, in a case reported by Bird (1981), a student wrote, "I would appreciate faculty advisor feedback regarding the quality of this nurse performance and specific opinion about the legal implications of health problems identified and not pursued."

Clearly, the clinical journal is an excellent evaluation tool to present the student's experiences, feelings, and questions. It is in fact the single most effective evaluative instrument and is of prime importance in providing the faculty member with the data needed to feel comfortable when students are working with clinical preceptors.

## ALTERNATIVES

In the preceding sections, we examined ways in which the professor can gain information and comfort about teaching students who are doing their clinical experience with another professional in a preceptorship role. In such a relationship, problems may still arise, and the professor may still

**Exhibit 8–1** Student Clinical Journal

---

*Date:* September 1, 1980

*Setting:* Adolescent Parent Program, Camelot High School District

*Activities:*

My time at the program was spent interacting with the clients and their children, including a mother whose two year old had acquired second degree burns on her foot the day before. I used the incident to point out to the mother that it was an ideal time to reinforce learning for "hot" by repeatedly pointing out such hazards and using the word "hot" while the pain of the accident is still fresh. Unfortunately, the use of the hot plate from which the child spilled hot water cannot be avoided. We talked about a better, safer placement for it, however. The child is receiving medical care and the mother is conscientious with treatment.

Conference with the teacher solidified direction in developing a plan for getting much needed attention to safety hazards on site. The teacher reports having filed numerous requests for such attention and has followed up with phone calls to the high school maintenance department—largely to no avail. The following four situations were given priority:

1. The large front window, which goes to the floor, is attractive to the toddlers, and the glass bows outward whenever a youngster leans on it.
2. The furnace is a wall type and goes to the floor on two walls; the surface gets too hot to leave the hand upon for more than 1–2 seconds.
3. The converted garage (used as a playroom) has an exposed hot water heater with a drain faucet adjacent to a laundry faucet that is 30 inches up the wall and is in close proximity to a live 220 volt outlet. There is a single wall outlet from which extension cords drape across shelves where toys are kept at lower levels and whose top shelf holds the small electric heater, the only source of heat in the room. The children have frequently gotten the water turned on—water stains are apparent for a large radius under both spigots.
4. Both front and back yards are high with weeds and grass. Only the back yard is fully fenced, but the children cannot use a small brick patio area for play because it contains a dismantled electric stove. Unfortunately, the oven door is about the only intact part and wiring springs from it in profusion. There is an accumulation of other "junk" items as well—including several boards and exposed nails.

The teacher and I briefly outlined what was needed to correct the hazards. Teacher will keep and add to the list. Student will request tactical advice from preceptor to motivate a response, as soon as possible, from the maintenance department.

Lunch permitted conference with preceptor, as well as introduction to the vice-principal. My report caught the attention of the latter (it seems that the adolescent parent program is under her "care") and, before I knew it, the head of maintenance was scheduled by the vice-principal to tour our site next week. A lengthy conference with preceptor followed, allowing an update of student activities and concerns and a sharing of methods and planning.

*Plan:*

Student will notify teacher of on-site maintenance visit and attend, to assist and reinforce identified needs. The vice-principal will join the tour as well.

*Time Spent:* 7½ hours

## Exhibit 8–1 continued

*Date:* September 8, 1980

*Setting:* Adolescent Parent Program, Camelot High School District

*Activities:*
Tour of the premises with vice-principal and administrator in charge of maintenance. This was very successful in that there were many clients and the toddlers did a beautiful job demonstrating safety needs, as they always do, by testing the environment and setting of limits. (Note: the recommended repairs and modifications were completed one week later, much to the joy and satisfaction of this student!)

*Source:* Bird, D. *Clinical journal.* Rohnert Park, Calif.: Sonoma State University, 1981.

## Exhibit 8–2 Weekly Student Journal

*Week 1:* I am feeling enthusiastic regarding my preceptorship. I feel confident that by having an excellent role model I will learn an incredible amount of information.

*Week 2:* I feel a bit overwhelmed and yet very curious to know and to understand more about the children I have seen today. I feel a real need to learn more so that I might be a valuable member of the health team.

*Week 4:* I did not realize I could fit so much into an afternoon. I realize the importance of organization, but also equally important, I must learn to be very flexible. I came home unbelievably exhausted.

*Week 6:* Whoever said school nursing was boring has not seen the likes of "Faufner School!"

*Week 7:* I am feeling frustrated at not being able to carry a task through from start to finish due to the number of drop-ins. The only solution I can see is to have two persons in the nurse's office, but then the office is so very small (the student's).

*Week 8:* Visit to "MAC Valley School." I am amazed at the differences between the "Faufner School" and the "MAC Valley School." I arrived home today feeling an incredible amount of frustration because not all schools are equal.

*Week 9:* I am feeling really good about what and how I am gaining knowledge in this preceptorship.

*Week 11:* At the present time I am functioning at Maslow's basic need level—one day at a time and surviving.

*Week 14:* This was a really tiring but satisfying day. I feel the lines of communication are now open between nurse, teacher, and parent.

*Week 15:* All in all, I definitely feel that my experience at "Faufner School" has been not only a very positive one for me, but also one of the best learning experiences I have had.

*Source:* White, V. *Clinical journal.* Rohner Park, Calif.: Sonoma State University, 1981.

be uncomfortable, despite all the remedies that may have been applied. In this case the sources of the faculty advisor's dis-ease and lack of comfort will most often be either (1) a personality conflict between student and preceptor, or (2) a change in the agency, its protocol, policy, staffing pattern, or location that cancels the preceptorship study. Now the faculty member is on the spot. In order for the student to have a meaningful preceptorship clinically, another preceptor or clinical agency must be found. If time is the problem, the student may elect to double the clinical time and complete it ahead of schedule. If it is the preceptor who is no longer available, the student may be able to transfer to another professional in the same agency who is qualified and willing to assume the preceptor role. Occasionally, the faculty advisor will need to transfer the student to a similar agency, preferably with a professional who has worked with preceptorship students before. These alternatives may create new, uncomfortable clinical situations, but there are usually means at hand to solve the attending problems.

## CONCLUSION

Preceptorship study is a clearly defined course of study. It meets the individual's needs and matches the student's interest so that identified professional goals can be achieved. The responsible academic faculty member can facilitate the total preceptorship experience by planning, teaching, counseling, and serving as an additional role model. By following certain procedures and developing appropriate attitudes, the faculty member can provide a meaningful clinical experience for the student and can feel comfortable when the student is doing clinical work guided by another person.

**REFERENCES**

Bird, D. *Clinical journal.* Rohnert Park, Calif.: Sonoma State University, 1981.

Freed, L., & Landis, C. *Developing contracts for preceptorship study.* Rohnert Park, Calif.: Sonoma State University, Department of Nursing, 1981.

McWhinnie, V. *Clinical evaluation.* Rohnert Park, Calif.: Sonoma State University, 1981.

White, V. *Clinical journal.* Rohnert Park, Calif.: Sonoma State University, 1981.

# Part II

# How It Feels To Be a Clinical Preceptor—The Preceptor Perspective

# Chapter 9

# Positive Aspects of the Preceptor Role

*Barbara A. Bergeron*

## NEW IDEAS AND CHALLENGES

Preceptoring in essence is teaching. To teach, one must know very well the material to be taught. This evolves into a learning process for both teacher and student. One of the most positive aspects in the role of preceptor is this learning-teaching process. It is a challenging and invigorating experience to have a student ask questions about things that have long been tangled, or even lost, in the recesses of one's mind.

Of course, we cannot all be specialists in every field. The health care field is constantly expanding. The technology grows increasingly sophisticated. Health care is now so diversified that it has become difficult for most of us to maintain expertise in more than one specialized area. Also, we do not come into contact with every type of situation, circumstance, or illness every day. We do not need all types of skills in everyday situations. However, you can bet that, at some point, a sharp student will come along and want to know about the very thing you have not seen or done in the past five years. In such a situation, trying to recall the correct information really joggles the brain cells and can be a real jolt to the preceptor's ego.

Yet, taking on the responsibility to help teach a student can be a positive and rewarding experience for both teacher and student, especially if the student is inquisitive. Often, students bring new and refreshing ideas, creating a new outlook on the community and environment. If inquisitive, the student will always be looking for ways to improve things. Such motivation may indeed resurface one's own goals that may long ago have become dormant due to lack of time and energy.

Many health care providers have been working in a particular area for a long time. Due to demands of work, and perhaps family, they often lose touch with developments at large medical centers and universities and some of the new trends in nursing/health care. It is often a long distance to stimulating continuing education programs, and the opportunities to attend such programs are infrequent. While reading helps, one cannot always monitor the new trends from such sources. In this situation, the student may give the preceptor an opportunity to learn some of the new trends that are developing in other areas.

## COMMUNITY INTERACTION

Another important positive aspect is community interaction. Most preceptors do not have the time to interact with the community as they would like. As a result, they lose insight into some of the basic community needs. They may also have an unrealistic view of the needs due to this lack of interaction at all levels of the community. The student can be the preceptor's link to the community in such situations.

An energetic student, new to the community, will look at things in a different light. The student can come up with ways to solve problems that had not been considered before, or may even discover some new problems. This may occur as the student is completing a project as one of the student's own goals.

As an example, perhaps the student's goal is to define a portion of the population in need of health care in relation to obstacles to that health care. The student may discover such problems as illegal aliens who will not use local health care facilities for fear of being turned in to the authorities. To remain anonymous, these people are traveling 50 miles to use an emergency room where they are unknown, and where they will not have to be seen again. The student may find other illegal aliens who are being preyed upon by their employers but who tolerate the abuse for fear of repercussions. Another frequently underserved population is the homebound elderly who cannot afford medical care and lack the transportation to go for help. They may also be blocked from signing up for tax-supported medical care due to the lack of transportation, or to the lack of local caring family members to help them. There is an unending list of similar conditions that the student may discover.

Most of us are aware of some of the inadequacies in our communities or hospitals, but not all of them. To effect changes, we must first be aware that a problem exists.

Many preceptors have goals for their community that they cannot meet due to lack of time, to overwork, or for other reasons. Such goals may include the establishment of screening clinics for seniors or children, teaching groups at need, home health care or assessment, organizing support groups, or starting a senior nutrition center. Sometimes help is needed to achieve such goals.

Again, an energetic, motivated student can take on one of these projects, get it started, and devote a lot of time and energy to doing it very well. What a positive accomplishment this can be for the student—especially if the student can look back two years later and see that the project is still functioning.

Tackling a project like this can also be a good motivating force for others, particularly if the community is lethargic. Someone lending an ear to and taking an interest in community needs is also good public relations for the preceptor and the organization the preceptor represents.

As students prepare to embark on this new type of learning experience in a totally new environment, they often have preconceived ideas of what the new locale will be like. Often, the area they will be living in during the preceptorship period is hundreds of miles from where they were raised. Sometimes they may have heard what it will be like from two or three other people, who may not really know either. Expectations and reality often clash harshly.

For example, someone raised in a large metropolitan area—with many hospitals, doctors' offices, parks, theaters, and grocery stores—may be shocked by going to a small, rural community of 2,000 people with industries of logging, farming, and ranching. Perhaps the nearest pharmacy is 30 miles away and the closest hospital is 50 miles away. The closest grocery store also may be many miles away. Similarly, a person raised in a small, rural community may have difficulty adjusting to an urban setting in a preceptorship experience. The new home may be very stressful for some people; others may in fact be unable to cope with such a drastic environmental change. Yet, for others, an environmental change can be a positive experience. We tend to take for granted the things that are provided us in our accustomed environment. Learning about alternative life styles can be stimulating and growth producing.

People who have lived in the same area all their lives tend to be set in their ways, unused to other life styles, and sometimes suspicious of people who act, look, or dress in different ways. The student must keep this in mind when living in a new area for a short while. The student may feel the same way about the old timers in the new area. The mutual experience may be very stressful if the student does not try to "fit in."

Yet, given a little time, suspicions wear down, and one will be accepted if one's attitudes are not inflexible. Humility is probably the best lesson a person can learn from such an experience. It is very humbling to arrive in a new place, see lots of things you want to change for the better (so you think), and then find out that no one else shares your excitement. The staff may be content with the way things are done.

## NEW SKILLS

In gaining new skills in a learning situation, we are ordinarily taught the ideal way of doing things, or the ideal way to perform them under certain circumstances. This often leads one to feel the need for changing things that do not fit the ideal. This is only natural. In reality, there is more than one way to do a job well. A student who is working under less than ideal conditions will learn to be inventive and adaptable. This can teach one tolerance, responsibility, and creativity and can also broaden one's viewpoint.

Some skills just take lots of practice before they can be performed well—such as starting IVs, placing catheters, changing dressings, or assessing trauma. A positive aspect for the student during a preceptorship program is the ability to try out hands-on skills. In large teaching institutions, the student nurse is often at the bottom of the hierarchy in attempting to use such skills. There is often a line of students waiting for the same chance.

In the preceptorship program, there is a one-to-one relationship. The preceptor usually needs the extra help of the student. There is often an abundance of patients and a shortage of help. The student may be called on to perform duties the student never would have imagined doing or to learn new skills never before considered. In such an environment, the student can gain a great deal of self-confidence and knowledge. Indeed, knowing that you have helped students gain confidence, experience, and the knowledge base needed to provide good nursing care to others is probably the utmost positive experience the preceptor will gain from the role.

## ACHIEVING OBJECTIVES

Other benefits to the student stem from the actualization or implementation of their objectives. Most students have spent days, if not weeks, developing objectives to accomplish during a short time spent in an unfamiliar place, while working with people they have never seen or talked to before. An overwhelming amount of stress and energy goes into this preparation process. The reward is in the successful completion of the preceptorship. In most instances, it is possible for the student to achieve this goal. Few fail in their efforts.

Goals or objectives usually include such things as defining the type of population served, evaluating or defining areas of need, learning about the referral services that are available, and learning to become proficient with a certain skill, such as physical assessment.

Occasionally there are goals that are just not possible to reach in a given setting. Part of learning to work with others is learning to compromise. This is an important lesson. By compromising in small ways, an alternative suitable to everyone can usually be found. And all parties concerned will be happier and more fulfilled from the experience.

Preceptors have goals, too. Examples are shaping student ideas to develop nursing skills the preceptor sees as desirable or encouraging students to relocate to an area of need. The actualization of the preceptor's goals is the reward, though again, in reality all of the preceptor's goals may not be fulfilled.

It is frightening to some people to change life styles—from the known to the unknown. Yet, in the last decade there has been a great and growing migration of population from large cities to rural and urban areas. Due to the resulting changes in population densities, the inability of schools to keep up with the growing need for trained personnel, and the lack of migration of health care providers to underserved areas, there will remain large areas of health manpower shortages, and health needs will grow.

Preceptoring can be viewed as a means to teach health care professionals how to deliver services in these areas, under new circumstances, as the imbalance of available services and perceived needs continues to grow. In the next 10 to 20 years, we will in fact see even greater changes in population densities, health care needs, politics, and crime, thus creating new avenues of health care practice.

## CONCLUSION

It is fascinating to think that one can be "in" on the development, at the ground level, of personnel who will be able to respond to the changing needs and requirements in the health care field of the future. Yet, in spite of good intentions, students and preceptors will sometimes experience clashes of ideals, goals, and expectations. Each will have their own preconceived ideas of the "perfect" preceptor or student.

It would be easy for a preceptor to design an ideal image of an outgoing, friendly, knowledgeable, well-dressed student. Students have similar images of the ideal preceptor. However, there are times when these images are far from reality. Remember that no one is liked by everyone and everyone is liked by someone. Though a student may not be the ideal person, that student still may be a perfectly capable person.

An important part of being a professional is the ability to get along with others. This is especially important in the health care field. The community where the preceptoring program is being utilized is the major beneficiary of this ability. First, someone is examining their needs with fresh insight and enthusiasm and trying to develop new or better ways to serve those needs. Second, new, experienced, and trained health care professionals are coming into contact with new areas, seeing possibilities for job prospects they had not considered before.

In the past, new nurses have generally stayed in the cities where salaries are higher, hospitals are better equipped, educational facilities are more numerous, and jobs are more secure. People have been afraid to venture into new, unknown areas. Now, preceptoring is bringing students to those areas that are not covered by conventional programs and that they would otherwise not have had an opportunity to see.

Thus, preceptoring is an important contribution that currently involved health care professionals can make. It is a positive role that one can play in shaping health care delivery and participating in future social change.

# Chapter 10

# What Precepting Is

*Claude T. Bergeron*

## BACKGROUND

Precepting in its simplest form means to teach. It is the passing along of knowledge or skills from one person to another. In the early days, when institutions of higher education in this country were few and far between, precepting was one of the most commonly used methods of acquiring skills past secondary school. As the country developed, so did its colleges and universities. They in turn took on the responsibility of training more and more of the professions. Today we have a system that takes two paths after graduation from high school. One is the now traditional college education and degree system. The other, a widely used path, is the apprenticeship system. This system utilizes an expert in the field who supervises and trains an apprentice for a specified length of time. Most of the crafts and building trades use this method. The college system gives a maximum amount of didactic information with very little hands-on experience. The apprenticeship programs have a great deal of hands-on experience. Only that didactic information that is necessary in the field is taught.

In the early days of nursing education, on-the-job training was primarily used to teach students. Slowly, nursing education moved from the hospital ward to the classroom. Today, many university programs are rediscovering the value of hands-on experience and are using elective nursing preceptorships to allow the nursing student an opportunity to experience the type of nursing they are interested in. Many nursing students under a preceptor arrangement are learning a wide variety of nursing skills. The learning sites vary from inner-city clinics, rural settings, specialized departments in large medical centers, to Indian reservations and migrant camps.

There are many ways to select a preceptor. Often, the university will contact an agency and make a request that it furnish a preceptor in a certain area. The nursing director will usually choose someone that fits the requirement. There are times, however, when the process is reversed and the request for a student comes from someone on the staff. In this case, the request usually goes to the director of nursing, who in turn contacts the college or university and requests that that facility be used in a preceptorship program for a student.

## REQUISITE QUALITIES

There are certain things to look for when choosing a preceptor. One of the most important is that the preceptor be a willing participant. Precepting a student requires a commitment of time and energy above and beyond the normal workload. If the preceptor is not willing to make this commitment, the quality of the student preceptor relationship will suffer. The preceptor must also be knowledgeable in the area that the student wishes to pursue.

Objectivity is also an important and desirable trait in a preceptor. We all have biases about people and events. These biases affect the way we behave toward others and how we react to situations. Not every preceptor will get a student that parallels that preceptor's concept of what a nursing student should be. The ability to remain objective and to respond objectively to those that meet our approval as well as to those that do not is a rare trait. The preceptor should be aware of these biases and strive to overcome any that will interfere with the relationship.

The relationship between preceptor and student is a give-and-take situation. The student also has something to give. A preceptor that does not learn something and grow somewhat with each student is missing a great deal.

From the preceptor's standpoint, it is helpful to know a little about the student's objectives before the arrival of the student. The preceptor presumes that the student is interested in the particular area of nursing or the student would not have asked for the experience. If the student can list the objectives that the student wishes to gain from the experience, the preceptor can give some thought as to how the objectives can be met in the most positive way. If the distance between the student and preceptor is not too great, a brief visit before starting the preceptorship can be of great value. Face-to-face contact is always best. Many students choose settings that are distant from the area where they live and go to school. For example, a nursing student in southern California may choose a setting in northern California. In such cases, a short phone call is helpful to work out last minute details.

The preceptor's expectations of what a student should or should not be will have a bearing on how the preceptor responds to him or her. For example: Imagine you are the only nurse on duty in a small rural hospital. Your entire staff consists of two nurse aides and yourself. You are also the preceptor of a nursing student. You may look upon your nursing student as a welcome 25 percent increase in staff.

As another example, imagine you are one of six public health nurses. Your county consists of small population centers scattered over a large area. You have one medium-size urban community in the county. Interspaced between the communities are rural agricultural areas. Your schedule is fast-paced. Distances between clinics and the time between visits are great. The logistics of your area of service pose major problems, and you are constantly faced with not enough time to perform your duties. In this case, you may view the student as just another problem to solve or another task to perform. The student in turn will certainly get a different view of nursing from this placement.

Perhaps you are a nurse practitioner in an independent setting. No services are available except from yourself. Medical backup is 60 miles away. No professional staff are available to support you. You have a front and back office assistant you had to train yourself. Your dream has been to have a back office RN to help you. In this case, your student will certainly be a welcome sight.

Based on your expectations and needs, you will thrust the student into some role that will suit your needs. However, remember that the student also has needs and expectations. As a preceptor, it is your responsibility to consider this in your decision. No matter how far apart the objectives of student and preceptor, there is some area in between that will be acceptable to both parties. Compromise is an art that must be learned and applied in order to be effective in this role.

In developing your philosophy to deal with the preceptor role, you should keep the following things in mind:

- Your nursing students have good backgrounds.
- For some students, the preceptorship is an elective.
- They are paying their own way, out of their own pocket, for the time they are with you.
- There is something they want to learn about nursing or they would not be there.

These attributes will eliminate the average student with only average interest. What you have left will be students with above-average interest, who are well-motivated and willing to pay to get what they want. Remember, the preceptorship program is designed to expose nursing students to specialized areas in nursing, with the expectation that some of them will return to work in those areas later on.

If you are a nurse preceptor in an area that has a chronic shortage of nurses, you have a great opportunity to "sell" your point of view. Keep your eye on the bottom line, which is to recruit future nurses.

## SETTLING IN

The day finally arrives and your first student is there. You have received in advance a copy of the student's application to the program along with a list of the student's objectives. Now is the time to sit down and let your student know what you and your site are all about. Go over the objectives and see how many of them will be able to be met with no problems. Firm these up so that the student can get started on them. Schedule another conference for a week later. This will give the student time to meet some of the easy objectives, to get settled in, and to think about some of the other objectives.

The second conference gives you a chance to discuss some of the objectives that do not easily fit into your site. In this meeting, you can determine some way to meet these objectives or to modify them to fit the situation.

Usually, the preselection process will have matched up the student and preceptor pretty closely so that the objectives are not hard to meet. The student who wants to go on to be a PHN in an inner-city area is usually matched up with the proper role model. The student who would like to become a nurse practitioner in the boondocks will get matched with someone who is working there.

However, there is always some unique situation that just does not fit the mold. Suppose you get a nursing student who says, "I want to find out everything I can about health delivery to the poor and minority groups in rural areas, how their care differs from that of other consumers, and how this is determined and by whom." In your first contact, you find out this student does not intend to practice nursing in a clinical setting. Rather, the student expects to become politically active and to try to influence health care legislation to improve health care delivery to poor and minority groups. Do not panic and do not laugh. Objectives like this are uncommon but must be dealt with. Part of your role as preceptor is to help meet these unusual needs. You were matched up with this particular student because the instructor felt you could handle the situation best, or your location offered the best chance of success in fulfilling the objective. This calls for inventiveness. You live in the area and know how the system works. You also know the politics of the area and the people to contact. Setting up the requisite experiences for the student can not only be fun; you may also learn something.

As a preceptor, you will see many unusual things happen. Some will be funny, and some will be sad. However, whatever your clinical setting is, it will be a change for the student. Sometimes it will be just a small change; sometimes it will be a large change. On some occasions, it will be a big cultural shock. The majority of nursing students are middle-class Americans from predominately urban areas. When they choose clinical settings that are inner city or rural, they are entering areas with which they are not only unfamiliar but of which they have little first-hand knowledge. People react to strangers in widely varying ways. People from inner-city, high crime areas react differently from those in rural areas, Indian reservations, migrant camps, and lumber communities. As a preceptor, it is part of your job to help prepare students in the roles that they must play while they are with you. Students who are flaming liberals in an ultraconservative community will not be very well accepted unless the preceptor has adequately prepared them for the situation and the students have modified their behavior accordingly.

These vast differences in backgrounds can be very stimulating for student and preceptor alike. Many students have discovered new hobbies, such as hunting and fishing, while on assignment. Others have discovered snow and ice storms for the first time. What does a person who is new to an area do when stuck in a snowbank for the first time, realizing it is 30 miles to the nearest community? Again, it is the role of the preceptor to foresee problem areas and adequately prepare the student to cope with them. Many students will be away from home, family, and friends for the first time in their lives. These students will look to the preceptor for guidance until they become accustomed to the new environment.

## THE EVALUATION PHASE

After the student has spent the required time at your site and has met the objectives that were laid out several weeks ago, your obligation is almost over. The most important part of the experience is now at hand— the evaluation.

Ideally, you have had regular meetings with your student and communications have been honest. The content of the evaluation should come as no surprise to anyone. The evaluation merely documents the experience so that others, such as instructors, can get official feedback. It is also a learning tool for both the student and the preceptor.

Evaluations usually involve various forms of boxes to check. They are designed for speed and efficiency. The best type of evaluation to give is a brief written note to let others know exactly how the student performed. This is more bother than making a check in a box, but it is worthwhile. After investing several weeks in a relationship with a student, it deserves more than just a check mark, and both students and instructors will appreciate the extra effort.

To someone new to making an evaluation of another person, the experience can be very stressful. There are some basic ground rules to follow to help ease the situation:

- You should strive to be as objective as possible. This is harder than it sounds. We all respond emotionally to others, positively or negatively. However, our emotional response may not be based on objective data. If the student reminds you of your aunt Mildred, whom you hate, the poor student will have an awfully hard time winning your approval.
- The evaluation can characterize the student in one of three ways: above standard, standard, or below standard. A standard evaluation means that the person shows up on time and performs all duties in a satisfactory manner. It implies satisfactory performance in all areas. An above-standard rating means that the person did something above and beyond what you would expect the person to do. A below-standard evaluation means that the person did not do something that was a usual and customary part of the expected performance. Any time you give an above- or below-standard rating, you are obligated to cite specific incidents, dates, and so on, to substantiate your claim. An unsubstantiated above- or below-standard rating should probably be thrown out by the reviewer of a performance rating.
- A performance rating should be confirmed by an independent reviewer. In the case of your student, the school of nursing will assign an instructor to be the reviewer.

Some of the positive traits to look for in students are initiative, neatness of person, sensitivity to others, and a good performance of skills. Negative aspects, which by the way are rare, are the reciprocals of the positive traits.

## CONCLUSION

Over the long haul, precepting will be a rewarding experience. Persons who are doing something they feel is worthwhile usually have no problem telling others about it. If you value what you are doing, the student will most likely value it also.

The goals of a preceptorship program are (1) to find preceptors in areas of nursing, (2) to place interested students with those preceptors, and (3) to involve students in the nursing experience. Hopefully some of the students will return to their preceptorship areas after graduation to serve the needs of the people there.

Someday you will open the mailbox and find a letter from a former student. The letter will tell you how the experience that that person shared with you influenced them in making a career decision. A letter such as this will likely be the biggest paycheck you will ever receive from anyone.

# Chapter 11

# The Needs of a New Preceptor

*Jane Henneman*

What it means to accept the role of a preceptor needs to be clearly defined. Many aspects of the preceptorship might be thought through after the role has been accepted. Yet, the role can be a valuable learning experience for both the preceptor and the student.

## DEFINING THE PRECEPTOR ROLE

The preceptor's needs and the student's needs must be identified prior to the beginning of the clinical experience. The role of the preceptor must be that of a facilitator of the student's goals and objectives. The preceptor must carefully review these goals and objectives, then revise them in the light of the clinical experience. Both the student and the preceptor must keep in mind that these goals and objectives are always in the context of the exposure to a new learning experience. The preceptor needs to evaluate how the goals and objectives can be met in the clinical surroundings. Prior to starting the learning experience, the preceptor must evaluate the course of the clinical experience. This must be done concurrently with identification of the preceptor's and student's needs. These needs can be met by carefully evaluating the goals and objectives, on the understanding that they are constantly changing during the exposure to the new clinical area.

After carefully evaluating the student's goals and objectives, the preceptor must analyze the health care facility's potential for a learning experience. Some questions must be asked:

- What can our facility offer to this student as a new learning experience? The facility may be unique in certain respects compared to other facilities.
- What background in clinical experience does the student have? The student may have prior experience clinically. The preceptor must be

aware of these past experiences and provide a unique clinical experience. In addition, many new ideas and experiences can be shared by the student.

- What is unique about the facility? The facility may have one or more specialties that the student might want to focus upon. The clinical experience may be entirely different from that experienced in the past.

- What is the relationship between the health care facility and the community? The community should be surveyed regarding its social structure—urban, suburban, or rural. Each of these types of communities is different in providing health care. The relationship of the community and the health care facility must be identified to provide a valuable learning experience.

- What are the objectives of the nursing service and the health care agency? These may help to define the role of the preceptor in providing a valuable learning experience for the student.

The preceptor can point out all these factors to the student. After carefully considering them, the preceptor will be better able to analyze the health care facility's potential to offer a valuable experience. The focus here must be upon the type of facility, the background of the student, the community relationship with the facility, and the objectives of the facility and the nursing service.

## PROJECTING THE PRECEPTOR ROLE

Another aspect of being a new preceptor is the projection of the role. First, the preceptor must have the attitude of a resource person rather than that of a supervisor or instructor. The preceptor should be available at all times to provide guidance for the student. The student will have many questions about procedures, policies, and rationales that will require feedback in certain situations. Second, the preceptor must also be flexible, allowing original goals and objectives to change as the student gains experience in the new environment. Learning experiences not originally identified as goals and objectives will be added. The preceptor must accept this flexibility in changing goals and objectives as the clinical experience progresses. This flexibility also applies to clinical time spent by the student in meeting certain identified goals and objectives. The student may want to survey the community, investigate outside resources, or investigate environmental factors.

Third, communication should be at the student's level and not at the preceptor's level. The preceptor should evaluate each student individually and not expect a knowledge base at the same level as that of the preceptor. Communication at the student's level will prevent misunderstandings. The preceptor should be aware at all times of the student's ability to understand. The preceptor must quickly recognize any misunderstanding and clarify what is to be communicated.

## IMPLEMENTING THE PRECEPTOR ROLE

When the preceptor understands the role, identifies goals and objectives, and evaluates the facility and possible learning experiences, the implementation of the preceptorship can begin. In implementing the preceptorship, the preceptor should keep in mind the factors we have outlined, to provide an objective onset of the preceptorship.

It is to the preceptor's advantage to become familiar with the student before the preceptorship is to begin. This can be done through questionnaires sent to the student. In these forms, the student provides information regarding prior experiences, expectations, social background, and educational background. This will help the preceptor become familiar with the student.

### Meetings and Orientation

Upon beginning the clinical experience, it is important to meet with the student face to face. At this time, the student can be oriented to the health care facility. A general tour can help identify new goals and objectives. This tour can also assist the preceptor and the student to become acquainted with each other. During the tour, the preceptor can introduce the student to the significant persons in the facility. This will help the student become familiar with the facility's general climate.

After the tour and introduction to significant personnel, the preceptor can meet again with the student to discuss the goals and objectives. The student can at this time more realistically identify how the goals and objectives can be met. It should be kept in mind, however, that these goals and objectives should be revised as the clinical experience progresses. The meeting with the student and the general orientation to the health care facility will assist the student in identifying new goals and objectives and in acquiring a general feel for the facility's social climate, thus making the student feel more comfortable.

During the clinical experience, the preceptor must assist during the student's rotation. The preceptor can do this primarily by providing proper guidance. Learning experiences and unusual events can be brought to the student's attention, keeping in mind the particular goals and objectives the student has identified. By keeping the student involved in the facility's programs and events, the preceptor will provide additional guidance.

## Feedback

During the rotation, it is important for the preceptor to provide continuous feedback. This can be done informally or formally. Feedback obtained informally can be on an irregular basis. It can be obtained at any time after a significant event takes place. For example, the preceptor may want to advise the student concerning new policies and procedures in the facility. Or the student may have questions regarding a policy or procedure. The preceptor must be available to provide this information with appropriate rationale. The preceptor can also utilize the informal feedback process in providing evaluation of the student's performance in a particular event. This feedback may help the student in future events.

Formal feedback may be easier to implement. A formal feedback process involves scheduled meetings between the student and the preceptor. Depending upon the length of the clinical experience, these meetings can be scheduled weekly. The topics discussed may involve whether the goals and objectives are being met, the student's clinical performance, and the student's peer relationships. The discussion must deal with past, present, and future goals and objectives. The reasons why goals and objectives have been identified, revised, or deleted must be discussed in order to get a clear understanding of the student's clinical experience. Discussion of the clinical performance involves professional projections, rationales for particular performances, and the health care facility's goals and objectives.

Peer relationships are a vital part of any clinical performance. They include not only those with the student's coworkers but also those with the student's clients. The student receives feedback not only from the preceptor but also from peers and clients. This information can be included in the formal feedback process between the preceptor and the student.

Not only does the preceptor give feedback, the student also provides feedback to the preceptor. The preceptor needs this information in order to improve the preceptor's role as a mentor. If the student's needs are not being met, the preceptor needs to be aware of this in order to effect changes. The preceptor must accept this feedback objectively, as positive criticism, in order to provide a valuable learning experience for both the student and the preceptor.

**Evaluation**

Upon ending the clinical experience, the preceptor needs to meet with the student in order to evaluate the entire experience. At this time many topics can be discussed. Primarily, the discussion should be directed at whether the final goals and objectives were met. The discussion can be focused upon how they were met and the events that led to the achievement of the goals and objectives. If the goals and objectives were not met, the reasons should be investigated.

The final evaluation should be focused upon the increased knowledge base obtained through the clinical experience. This can make the preceptor and the student aware of the uniqueness of the clinical experience. Finally, the entire experience must be discussed in relation to how it will affect the student's future career. The impact of the experience will affect future clinical performance, thus adding to the student's general knowledge base.

**CONCLUSION**

The role of a preceptor can provide a valuable learning experience for the preceptor as well as for the student. The role must be clearly defined prior to beginning the preceptorship. Descriptive goals and objectives must be identified by the student. These goals and objectives must be specific for the health care facility in which the clinical experience will take place.

The preceptor's role must be projected with the attitude of a resource person. Flexibility must be allowed in changing goals and objectives and in determining how they are to be met. Communication must be at the level of the student. The preceptor must become acquainted with the student prior to beginning the clinical experience.

At the beginning of the experience, a face-to-face orientation meeting should be held between the student and the preceptor. The preceptor must provide proper guidance throughout the entire clinical experience, during which continuous, informal and formal feedback is exchanged between the student and the preceptor. Arrangements must be made for periodic meetings with the student to exchange valuable feedback. A final evaluation session must be held by the student and the preceptor at the end of the clinical experience. These factors are all-important in considering the needs of the new preceptor.

# Chapter 12

# The Challenge of Being a Preceptor

*Jeannie B. Maes*

Webster defines a preceptor as a "teacher, instructor, tutor . . . a specialist in a branch of medicine or surgery who takes a young physician as a resident student and gives him personal training in his specialty (1961, p. 1784). The preceptor, as discussed in this chapter, is a nurse who has expertise that has been gained in one health area from experience and study over time. It is possible for a nonnurse professional to act as a preceptor. (In the present context, a professional is defined as a person who consistently expands a knowledge base involving a current practice and the state of that person's specific field of expertise.) Examples would be a teacher in a preschool program, an agency health educator, a staff person in a senior citizens center, or a private health practitioner. The nonnurse preceptor has a special challenge in understanding the role, function, limits, and expertise of nurses. The students of such a preceptor could be nurses expanding their knowledge base or student nurses preparing themselves more broadly in a particular area of interest before becoming licensed. The nonnurse practitioner has an ethical and legal responsibility to work closely with the nurses from the school and/or placement agency.

The professional nurse who assumes the role of preceptor for advanced student nurses or nurses returning for further education is one who has shown excellence in a field of nursing. The willingness to share implies a high degree of self-motivation, innovativeness, responsibility, and caring. In our experience, the same applies to the students of such nurses.

## PRECEPTOR MODELS

Three different preceptor models may be distinguished. In each, it would be possible to have the preceptor working with more than one student, for example, with a few students assigned to a coronary care unit. The staff could share the responsibility of the preceptorship and rotate work days, whereas the students could not. We would recommend a one-to-one relationship, however. This avoids all types of communication problems. Because the experience is usually quite time-limited, fewer variables should provide a clearer and more concise learning experience.

In the first model, the student may be placed with the preceptor in an agency the student has experienced before. The school monitors the placement. The preceptor and school therefore have a close communication process:

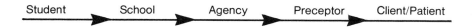

In the second model, a third agency arranges for, and monitors, the placement by the school. This placing agency negotiates with the school, student, community agency, and preceptor. The agency communicates less often with the clients, and the preceptor communicates less directly with the school:

In the third model, a school staff person with particular expertise in one area acts as preceptor and assists the student to accomplish the student's goals:

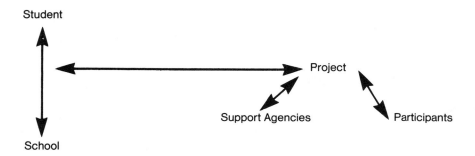

A fourth possible working relationship between individuals involved in a preceptor-student experience is more complex:

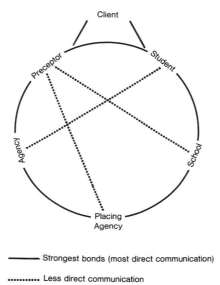

————— Strongest bonds (most direct communication)

·········· Less direct communication

## ROLES AND OBJECTIVES

The roles of a preceptor are multiple, involving three general levels. The most obvious is that of agency employee. The agency and preceptor must have a positive working relationship. The preceptor should be seen as a valued member of the staff. This individual must be knowledgeable and in general in agreement with agency goals, programs, and policies. The objective here is to assist the student to become acquainted with the agency itself. As the relationship progresses, the preceptor will demonstrate a professional role. The objective at this level is to act as a positive influence in enhancing the student's preparation for practice.

The role model is not limited to that of employee and professional, however. The third level involves the unique preceptor-student relationship. In some instances, the student may be living away from family and friends in a new community, in addition to experiencing a new agency and staff, and perhaps a new nursing role. The preceptor may add to the student's experience by sharing the preceptor's self as a person. Besides being part of an agency, the preceptor may thus be part of a family, community, or organization that can be shared with the student.

## PRECEPTORSHIP PHASES

After the model roles and objectives have been established, the experience begins. Four phases of the relationship may be distinguished. The length of each phase depends on the individuality of the preceptor and student and the length of time the student is with the preceptor. To make the preceptorship most enriching, we feel that all four phases should be experienced.

### Introduction and Establishment of Trust

This phase may progress quickly because of probable personality similarities, as noted earlier. In this phase, a general but clear idea of the agency goals and policies, staff characteristics, clients and patients served, and preceptor job description should be conveyed. Brief personal data are shared. Information as to the availability of preceptor and the preceptor's role in assisting the student is essential. Information on the student's general goals, expectations, and background should be obtained. Introductions to some staff and a brief tour of the agency may be made. During the first hour, the student and preceptor will be taking impressions and making judgments of each other. The preceptor may want particularly to assess the student's level of anxiety and interest in the assignment. Helpful behaviors to assist in the development of a sense of trust may include being able to convey the idea that the student is being listened to, explaining things briefly and concisely, and giving small amounts of information until the student seems ready for more. It is also important to display that intangible feeling of acceptance and caring by being at the appointment on time, by establishing eye-to-eye contact, by having an open, friendly attitude, by arranging for as few interruptions as possible, and by having a plan for orientation (then or later).

The student may come with written goals. In our experience, such goals are usually too global and general. During the initial meeting, more specific interests may be elicited. The first meeting may be brief or lengthy. If brief, it may be helpful to provide written information about the agency, pertinent policies, the professional's job description, and general information about clients. A time limit during which the packet is to be read and returned should be set. This helps to focus anxiety by giving a task at which the student can succeed, and it ensures a rapid, in-depth orientation.

An appointment for the next meeting or task should be made. Appropriate attire and what equipment or supplies to bring should be discussed. Finally, the all-important schedule of coffee breaks, lunch, and "quitting time" should be arranged. If time permits, the second phase (orientation/

supervision) may be started. In any case, the provision of written material for the student is highly recommended. This gives the student an opportunity to learn using another sense and does not take away from the preceptor's time with the student.

**Orientation and Supervision**

The goals and objectives of the student may be general at this time. The goals and objectives of the preceptor must be specific. The preceptor, who is knowledgeable about the agency and clients as well as the student's preparation, must lead the student in definite directions. These directions will stem from the student's academic preferences. The first learning experiences for the student will be building blocks on which to choose more specific goals and objectives during the third phase.

Now, a more concise orientation occurs. Arrangements are made for the student to talk with specific staff members, become acquainted with different agency departments, and develop an orientation to related agencies. Meetings with specific clients and patients and their families may now occur. The student will be led to specific library sections and become oriented to the community at large.

The amount of time spent with specific staff or clients and patients directly relates to the student's goals. Selected references, articles, and pamphlets giving more appropriate information and detailed information may be shared early in this phase.

The preceptor's role in the second and third phases may be differentiated in terms of the degree of directiveness or assertiveness assumed by the preceptor. The extent of this directiveness or assertiveness is greater in the second than in the third. However, the preceptor acts as a role model throughout the entire placement.

**Acting As a Role Model and Counselor**

At this point, the student has a much more solid base from which to make decisions regarding clients and patients. The student understands agency policy, protocol, and programs and has an increased nursing/medical knowledge and experience. Now, the preceptor and student should be communicating well. The preceptor has had opportunities to receive feedback regarding the student's comfort with the experience, knowledge, preferences for working areas, special interests, and ability to work with less supervision. Using this information, the preceptor now can assist the student to decide upon specific goals and objectives for the remainder of the experience.

The role of the preceptor at this time may be unique to the teacher-learner experience. The experience at this point may be more in-depth, intense, and broadening than any other the student will have. There may be, for the first time, the opportunity to make independent nursing judgments. In the second phase, the preceptor's energy was used to direct the student. Now that energy is spent assisting the student in solving problems and making independent judgments and plans. In this phase, the decision making is shared.

The student has observed the preceptor as a role model relate to colleagues and other staff members, practice nursing expertise, relate to staff of other agencies, work with family and clients or patients, function in society, and both teach and supervise. Now the student will observe the counseling role, one in which the preceptor allows the student to grow independently, to develop, and to use a new repertoire of skills. To be most effective, the preceptor must have the capacity to allow the student to develop some sense of autonomy.

Feelings experienced by the preceptor at this time may include fear, resentment, uncertainty, and loss. There might be a fear of student failure that would pose a safety problem for the client or patient or reflect a lack of capability in the preceptor. The lack of community acceptance of the student might also engender fear. Discomfort with a lack of student dependence, the possibility of student success where the preceptor has failed, or the setting of unrealistic goals may cause preceptor resentment of the student. Uncertainty about what the student is doing or how problem solving is proceeding could also cause the preceptor concern. A loss may be felt as the relationship with the student changes.

The distinctive experience of the third phase is at the crux of the challenge for the preceptor. Nevertheless, the preceptor should not stop guiding the student to new, unusual, or enhancing experiences that the student may not yet be aware of, for example, special work days or conferences, consultations with specialists, team meetings, or unusual presenting problems of clients or patients.

## Termination and Evaluation

At the end of the experience, the student may evaluate self, the preceptor, the experience, and possibly also the agency or project. The preceptor has the same opportunity. The preceptor's evaluation of self may include preparation to perform as preceptor in general and for this student in particular, timeliness of the shift from one phase to another (particularly from the second to the third), the preceptor's attitude regarding the student and the experience, the preceptor's availability to the student, and the preceptor's ability to help formulate appropriate goals and objectives.

Evaluation of student may be formal or informal. Formal evaluation may be requested from the school, placement agency, or participating agency. This may be accomplished by a combination of discussion and written evaluation, with each party using standard forms. Informal evaluation may have started early in the experience. Such evaluation is usually accomplished by discussion and, in our experience, is often initiated by the student.

The preceptorship experience can most easily be evaluated by reflecting on the student's goals and objectives and how and if they were accomplished. The experience from the preceptor's perspective can be similarly judged. The smooth transition from one phase to another, especially from the second to the third phase, could be reexamined. After the second phase, the preceptor could look at how goals were developed during the first two phases and accomplished during the third. During "slow" times, how creative were the student and preceptor in maintaining an intensive learning experience?

Evaluation of the agency or project may be appropriate and may indeed be requested by the placing agency or school. Items to consider might include appropriateness for student placement, receptiveness, value of the project, and community receptiveness.

Termination in a sense occurs at the end of each of the four phases. A clear, final termination of the experience may assist the student to begin the everchanging transition from the dependent role of a student to that of a competent professional.

The four phases of the preceptor-student relationship are shown in Figure 12–1.

## CONCLUSION

After all this—why be a preceptor? From the student's point of view, the preceptorship will probably be seen as an enriching experience of "real life" situations in which theory can be translated into practice. It may be an opportunity to gain self-confidence in making nursing judgments and interventions. The agency has the opportunity of giving an in-depth orientation. The student may become part of the staff or referring community.

From the community's perspective, the student may provide a special relationship with the client or patient. It may help professionals to see the humanness of the client, which we think should be a major goal.

The student may have an opportunity to observe how this special population and the community at large relate to each other. The total expe-

**Figure 12–1** Four Phases of the Preceptor-Student Relationship

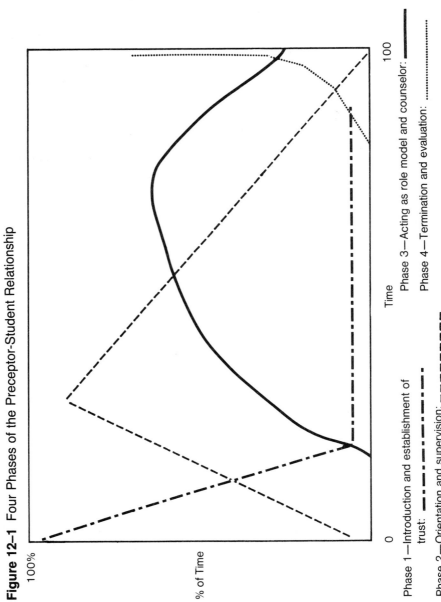

Phase 1—Introduction and establishment of trust: — ·· — ·· — ··

Phase 2—Orientation and supervision: — — — — —

Phase 3—Acting as role model and counselor: ──────

Phase 4—Termination and evaluation: ···············

rience will provide a broader decision-making base where the graduate works or resides.

Finally, the preceptor will find the experience personally enriching, may have an opportunity to share an area of special clinical interest, and will, with the student, view the experience as one of becoming part of the larger community and knowledgeable about the health concerns of a special population. The information obtained from the program could be used to determine if a need exists to modify the student's basic curriculum regarding the population served by the agency or project.

The need to balance the demands of the agency, the needs of the student, and the time involved, together with the demands of preparing for the broader role of being a preceptor, probably without monetary reward, is in itself a challenge. Add to that the need to facilitate the experience for the student, the agency staff, clients and patients, the family, and the related agencies' staff, and one has quite a task.

Is the preceptor able to accept the challenge of the role and be open to the student, accepting new knowledge and ideas? Elements of the total experience may, in some cases, put the preceptor in an adversary/competitor role. The school may have unrelated demands and agendas for the student that may be disruptive. Assignments and requests to return to the school may significantly decrease the time with the student. The placing agency may have assignments that take priority over the basic preceptor-student relationship and goal accomplishment. The agency, not recognizing the importance of the experience, or failing to support the project, may lack responsiveness to the student's needs. Still, if the profession is to continue to mature and meet the everchanging demands of society, preceptors must continue to perform their roles, thereby contributing that absolutely necessary quality of expertise to the new professional.

**REFERENCE**

*Webster's Third New International Dictionary.* Springfield, Mass.: G.C. Merriam Co., 1961.

# Part III

# Reality-Oriented Clinical Nursing—The Student Experience

# Chapter 13

# How a Preceptor-Based Clinical Experience Is Different from a Traditional Clinical Placement

*Monica Jean Davis*

## INDEPENDENT GROWTH

Traditionally, the clinical experience of a student nurse takes place in a hospital, clinic, or office with the preceptor or instructor always in attendance. The student can turn to the preceptor at a moment's notice for ready solutions to simple or complex problems. There is little independence in decision making or real experience with patients, staff, or family. The student is often not a part of the interaction that so often takes place when grave decisions must be made concerning treatment, such as whether surgery should be performed, whether to reinstitute chemotherapy, or when and how to inform a patient and family of a terminal illness. These are real-life situations that traditional clinical experience so often leaves out. Yet, in the real world of nursing, when the new nurse is expected to answer difficult questions posed by terrified and often angry patients, the new nurse becomes aware of a lack of experience.

Traditionally, student nurses wear colored uniforms and therefore stand out from the rest of the staff. They are not really considered part of the team. They are allowed to have team conferences, but all concerned know they are just "practice," and usually they are not taken seriously. They pass medication under their instructors' eyes and license. Each decision they make concerning patient care is evaluated and changed according to a staff and/or an instructor's opinion. They are taught team leading, but no primary care nursing, even though many hospitals are now completely or partially primary care facilities. Traditional clinical experience of student nurses in the second year or higher is unrealistic and unimaginative, with little opportunity to experience reality before they must assume responsibility for human life in addition to administrative duties, such as assisting and evaluating staff.

## CLOSER INTERPERSONAL RELATIONS

Another aspect of nursing that is sorely missed in traditional teaching is interpersonal relations. The students do not receive adequate practical experience relating to communication skills and techniques for managing interpersonal conflicts. Once the student nurses have made the transition to graduate nurse, they must deal directly with a variety of people, each of whom has a different motivation and set of expectations associated with the job. They will find some nurses supportive and caring, others indifferent and careless. They will experience moments of deep frustration and despair, and moments of unbelievable joy and fulfillment. As student nurses, they are often protected from or unaware of these experiences. Thus, they miss the feel and full impact of the various interpersonal situations they will encounter later in their careers.

In a preceptor-based experience, the student nurses meet a preceptor and discuss some basic goals, outline plans of learning, have ideas of what experiences they would like to have and proceed from there. They will obtain the preceptor's phone number at home and work. But as they proceed to the area of assignment, they begin to take their first big step toward functioning as a registered nurse—a skilled, professional, yet feeling, human being. Now, they no longer have an instructor at their side. They must utilize the personnel that are present when in need or doubt. They must be unafraid to ask questions and seek help from the nurse's aide or the nursing director.

If the students are relocating for their preceptorships, arriving at the new residence represents the first of many interactions between themselves and strangers. They must learn to establish new relationships. Without the security of friends, family, and familiar settings, this can be very difficult. Discovering the simple rule—be yourself—may take a few days or weeks. Discovering the other simple rule—allow others to be themselves—may take longer. But if they realize that we all share basic needs and desires, they will soon be able to handle the conflicts that arise with growth. Everyday living, with all of its inevitable misunderstandings, joys, and stresses, must be experienced and enjoyed independently by the students. They will either grow up very fast or become very distraught.

## NEW ALTERNATIVE APPROACHES

The assigned clinic setting may look alien at first glance. The students arrive full of ideals and innovative suggestions. They meet the stern faces of people who have worked there for 10, 20, or 30 years—people who say,

"We have done it this way for years, and it is good enough." Or, "Oh, he is just faking it, he doesn't need the pain medication yet." Or, "Don't disturb the doctor over that, this problem can wait until the morning." Or, "Of course he's dying, but we aren't going to tell him." Or, "He's just an Indian, they can take more pain." Or, "No, she is not spitting up blood, she chews tobacco." Or, "She's been here forever; they'll never fire her, no matter what she does or doesn't do."

How the students handle such prejudice, lack of concern, superficial judgments, lack of understanding, and all the other problems they will face will pave the way for growth. Yes, they must learn to accept the personalities and situations they encounter, and yet they must also learn how to introduce changes when necessary. They may have better techniques, new ideas, or alternative approaches to problem solving, but it is the way they present their case that will determine the reception and implementation. The student nurses will learn very quickly that they will make no progress by alienating those around them. It is important to listen and observe, to seek friendships with those they feel comfortable with and a truce with those with whom they do not. This will teach them that people are a product of their own particular experience and environment. They are not vicious or cruel by purpose or design. They are being themselves, judging patients by their own standards. They have not been to a seminar by Kubler-Ross. They have not acted out their emotions in a nursing school drama. They have rather been very busy living their own lives in their own realities, which may be very different from the students' realities.

## NURTURING STUDENT-PRECEPTOR RELATIONSHIPS

The students may need to meet with the preceptor to express frustrations. Well-informed preceptors can give motivation and confidence after they have allowed a student to cry on their shoulders. Even leaving the experience for a weekend can be healthy. Hopefully, this may relieve enough stress so that a student returns with a new perspective and renewed strength.

In a preceptor-based experience, students have set certain goals and objectives, and they also have the emotional inputs and changes needed to fulfill those objectives. The preceptor should discuss these goals and the progress being made at some point at the beginning, in the middle, and near the end of the experience. Then if the goals are unrealistic or impossible to fulfill, they can be changed and adjusted before the experience is over.

In fulfilling their goals and learning to make necessary changes in them, the student nurses will increase their ability to make decisions and take charge. They will have made important strides in becoming a professional. They will have freedom and yet security, functioning independently with the knowledge that the preceptor is available. If they feel real trouble is coming, they have a contact they can trust. They will learn to use their own judgment in discriminating between situations they can handle alone and those that require assistance.

The students should be encouraged always to discuss any difficulties, resolved or not, with their preceptor. In this manner, alternatives and options can be talked over. The students can see other ways to handle situations in the future. They should be congratulated if they handle a problem well on their own, and be assisted in working through a failure. The skilled preceptor will be able to anticipate a student's response fairly well halfway through the experience and will know which method works best with each individual. Not all students are ready for the independence and stress that are integral components of the preceptorship. As with all students or new graduates, some will stumble at first, then learn to adjust to the pace and the demands. Others will stumble through the entire experience. These people will need more guidance. The preceptor must be attuned to the needs of each student in their initial meeting and the meetings thereafter. Problems will crop up fairly soon with students who will need additional help. Occasionally, it may be necessary to withdraw a student from the experience. This is a very painful decision that should be thoroughly thought out and discussed with the student.

During the preceptorship, the students may find themselves confronted with people in many difficult and frightening situations—the terminally ill patient who is ready to discuss death and chooses the student as a confidant, those who have abortion by choice, rape victims, victims of child abuse, dying patients to whom the students feel close. They may find themselves participating in a code blue, helping a seizure victim, dealing with homosexuality in patient/staff, or confronting a suicidal patient. The students may have had previous experience with some of these situations, but the ability to handle each situation independently is the true test. The students are there with the patient and the family. It is up to them to comfort, support, explain, act as a patient advocate, and give of themselves as they may never have had to in their lives. No time to read up on how to handle a family who has just lost their 22-year-old daughter, wife, or sister to Ewing's sarcoma. No time to call the preceptor to ask if it is all right to cry with these people. They will determine for themselves if they will allow it to happen. And they will emerge a great deal stronger and better able to cope and care.

Hopefully, they will become aware that the real world of nursing is all about caring. Yes, they need good skills and the ability to start intravenous drips, recognize vital changes in a patient's condition, give emergency aid, and organize and assign staff members. But primarily they are givers of care in a caring way. Nurses take care of people. In a preceptor-based experience, student nurses can learn this before they are on their own in the hospital.

## EVALUATION LEADING TO GROWTH AND NEW RESPONSIBILITIES

As the students reach the climax of their experience, it is time to recount and evaluate. This is the time when the preceptor can be most helpful and can give some important input. Each student should be allowed to be with the preceptor from one to four hours, depending on the individual. The students need to evaluate and clarify particular episodes and moments and to discuss the value of the clinical experience. Sometimes the session may need to be repeated a month or more after the students have returned to their homes. The preceptor should be open to this possibility. Such sessions may contribute to an important growth process for some individuals who need to think over all that has happened and then talk more with the person who shared the experience with them.

For students who are prepared to accept responsibility and independence, the preceptorship experience is rich with opportunities to improve these skills and gain confidence as professional nurses. By being forced to cope independently with unfamiliar environments, personalities, and cultures, the student nurses will experience personal growth and maturity that will be tremendously rewarding.

# Chapter 14

# Positive Aspects of Working with a Preceptor

*Laura Deluca Douville*

## BACKGROUND

From the time of its conception, the nursing profession has been an everexpanding network. Nursing education is in a constant state of flux. It is continually studied and manipulated in order to create training programs that are adequate to meet the demands of a dynamic profession. The clinical education of nurses in training has always had loosely defined standards. Such education is considered to be an essential and integral element in the nurse training program, yet its claims are not absolute.

Clinical education has attracted much speculation and controversy throughout the history of nursing. Its value as a teaching and learning vehicle is subject to many variables, the most obvious of which is the availability of adequate patient care experiences necessary to learn, develop, demonstrate, and evaluate bedside nursing skills.

The first education program for nurses in the United States was an apprenticeship program. All the teaching and learning was done at the patient's bedside, with the more experienced nurse performing the duties of instructor in addition to duties as an employed nurse. Nursing education consisted solely of working in the hospital setting. Thus, hospitals that established schools of nursing benefited from inexpensive, eager, and productive students as workers. They were thus guaranteed a labor force of experienced, employable nurses when the student nurses graduated at the end of their year-long course.

Many nursing schools later expanded their programs from one to two years in length. Senior nursing students were designated as head nurses, responsible for the education of first-year students. Nursing education at this point depended on the dedication, knowledge, and skills of the individual nursing student-instructors and on the time available for the actual learning of nursing theory and practice, separate from the time spent completing unrelated hospital chores.

As nursing education came under closer scrutiny, it became apparent that the apprenticeship program had several drawbacks. Nursing students had become a source of cheap labor for hospitals to abuse. There was little time for skill development. There were few opportunities for the acquisition of theoretical knowledge to enable nursing practice to acquire a scientific basis. As nursing evolved from simply a barrage of varied tasks into a search for identity as a profession, a concern for the quality of nursing education was brought to the forefront.

Around the turn of the century, the Johns Hopkins School of Nursing initiated the move out of the hospital and into the classroom. Thus, nursing education became a didactic teaching and learning experience. Nursing arts instructors were appointed to teach procedures and to supervise demonstrations and practice in the classroom setting.

The emphasis on academic education grew. Gradually, an increased proportion of time was spent learning at the chalkboard rather than at the bedside. As this trend continued, student morale faded, and the pendulum swung in the opposite direction. Students lost interest as patient contacts and hands-on experience decreased. There was less opportunity to observe directly and to evaluate the signs and symptoms of illness. With more time removed from the hospital, a distinct dichotomy emerged between the ideal situation learned in the classroom and the real conditions one would be confronted with in the work setting.

In 1919, the National League of Nursing Education recognized the need for an improved clinical learning experience for young trainees. And so again, the emphasis swung back to clinical education. The concept of a clinical teacher as an entity separate from the academic instructor and separate from the ward nurse was proposed. This new role took on varied titles, from teaching supervisor in 1922, to ward instructor in 1926, to our own clinical instructors or clinical specialists of today.

As the nursing profession continues to grow and expand, new needs and demands are being faced. Nursing educators are being challenged to improve and upgrade training programs in order to produce quality nurses equipped with an increasingly complex combination of skills and knowledge to meet the expectations of a multifaceted profession. We have seen nursing education evolve from an apprenticeship teaching tool, to a classroom-based training program, to a system better balanced as a dyad of academic and clinical training.

The student in training was once considered to be a viable member of the work force and also a teacher of other students who had less experience, in addition to functioning as a pupil learning advanced skills. When the studies moved away from the wards and into the classroom, demands on the student to function in numerous, different roles decreased. However, fewer patient contacts meant a less personalized approach to patient care and, thus, less satisfaction to the student.

Nursing education today recognizes the fundamental need for quality education in both the clinical and academic setting. However, the correct ratio, the proportion of each that is necessary to create the optimum learning environment, varies according to one's frame of mind.

## ADVANTAGES OF A PRECEPTOR TEACHING PROGRAM

As nursing continues to become more specialized, as technology continues to grow in complexity, nursing education may revert to a more clinically oriented mode of teaching and learning. This is evidenced in the various preceptor teaching programs in operation today. These programs involve individuals who are knowledgeable and experienced in their line of work and who work with students and function as clinical instructors in the work setting.

### Workable Preceptor-Student Ratio

Thus, we return to a modified apprenticeship learning system. This method of learning has many advantages. One advantage is a very comfortable and workable preceptor-student ratio. The learning groups are small and, many times, direct one-to-one teaching is maintained. The student is in the enviable position of receiving personalized instruction. More energy can be spent in the teaching of skills and in the reinforcement of learning to meet the needs of the individual student. The student-teacher relationship remains flexible, and goals are discussed and defined by both parties. The objectives and goals may be written down, referred to, reevaluated, and redefined throughout the course of instruction, depending upon new needs that may arise or those needs that may change. The preceptor and student, through mutual discussion and agreement on set objectives and goals, enter into a partnership—each with different and distinct responsibilities but each with the same commitment—to work toward the established goals. Thus the traditional student-teacher relationship is transcended, and an interaction emerges that is marked more by unity and less by disparity.

As a learning experience, the possibilities are endless—this is the beauty of the ideal preceptor teaching program. If the student is energetic, assertive, and eager to learn, if the preceptor is receptive, resourceful, and willing to share knowledge and expertise, and if both persons harbor creative and intuitive minds, both student and preceptor will reap valuable benefits from the time and energy invested in the search for knowledge.

The student and preceptor maintain a close working relationship. Throughout the learning course, the student receives and incorporates messages concerning the preceptor's work role. Continued observations and constant verbal and nonverbal clues aid the student in forming and understanding the role function of the preceptor. The student has the unique opportunity of indirectly experiencing the preceptor's role. The student observes what is expected of the preceptor and how the preceptor functions in a variety of situations. The preceptor acts not only as an instructor but also as a role model for the student.

**Hands-On Experience**

The student also benefits from learning in the work setting. Hands-on experience immensely reinforces one's learning. By learning and working in one setting, the student is able to study, to observe, to demonstrate, and then to evaluate new academic and clinical concepts without the delay involved when students must travel from classroom to hospital room. Often in the preceptor teaching program there is immediate reinforcement of learning due to available clinical practice on hand.

While learning skills, the student is also learning to adapt to the work environment. Gradually, role functions specific to the skills being learned are incorporated into the learning experience. The student gradually acquires parts of the preceptor's role, facilitating the change in self-image from that of student to that of a health professional. The student adapts self-image and role expectations and incorporates the student's own perceptions into the preceptor's role. This is a major motivating factor. To be able to work toward and actually see oneself in a certain role is at the same time rewarding and inspiring. Students expend much time and energy and endure many sacrifices in their quest for advanced learning, development, and greater employment opportunities. The integration of one's self-image and one's role perception is essential in initiating goal-directed professional development. Achievement of this critical point is facilitated through a close working-learning relationship, which is an integral part of the preceptor teaching program.

**Interpersonal and Community Relationships**

The student also learns to develop and maintain working relationships with persons, other than the preceptor, who are essential in order to maintain and perform the student's role functions. The student develops communication and interactional skills and learns the politics involved with the people and place in which the student is learning and working. Networking skills may also be acquired. This is unique to an apprenticeship-type program in which the student becomes an integral part of the working community. The opportunity to learn and develop all these skills enhances job placement for the student at the completion of the training.

In an ideal preceptor teaching program, the student becomes involved not only in the work environment but also in the community as a whole. The student is encouraged to take part in community functions, attend town meetings, learn the history of the community, and get in touch with its people and their life styles. By becoming an active participant in the community, one can better appreciate the clients one is interacting with and caring for in the clinical setting. This enables the student to learn the holistic approach to assessment and to put this new skill into practice. Thus, factors such as socioeconomic status, cultural influences, demographic aspects, and forms of work and recreation can all be taken into account when attempting to plan a comprehensive health care program for an individual patient. The holistic approach encourages the treatment of a patient as an individual, as a unique sum of many interrelated parts.

**Direct Involvement**

Removed from the security of the classroom, the student working with a preceptor is confronted with an honest exposure to a real work situation. Opinions concerning work, its benefits, its salary, and its opportunities for advancement are formed by direct experiences in the work setting, not as something discussed in a classroom. The dichotomy between the ideal condition that is taught and the conditions that are actually faced in the work setting is thus not as glaring in a preceptor teaching program. The student learns and practices in the actual clinical setting. Even though, in theory, procedures and care plans are presented as ideal, the students in these programs have the opportunity of applying their knowledge as they learn it in true work situations. They learn firsthand the various influences that come into play and can alter ideal circumstances, working conditions, patient compliance, and presentation of signs and symptoms.

Problems such as poor staffing, low wages, long hours, poor working conditions, and so on, become apparent to the student who is working and learning in the clinical setting. The student is afforded the opportunity to see how such work-related problems are managed and how change is initiated and thus may learn and develop skills that can be used to become an effective change agent in the student's own future career.

All in all, the adjustment from functioning as a student to fulfilling a role as a health care professional would seem to be less traumatic for a young trainee who graduates from an apprenticeship-type learning program. There would be less disparity between the role expectations of the new graduate and those of the institution at which the graduate will be employed. If adjustments to the work situation are facilitated early in the student's career preparation, the student-graduate is likely to find the new job more rewarding, a vehicle that can be used for the continued learning of skills—clinical, academic, or managerial. As long as the new job does not have built-in roadblocks, the possibilities for continued acquisition and expansion of skills and knowledge are boundless.

## CONCLUSION

Throughout nursing's history, nursing educators have been hard-pressed to redefine and reconstruct nursing programs. New advances in technology, new breakthroughs in medicine, require a highly trained, highly skilled nurse in the patient care setting. Traditionally, the education of nurses has consisted of two teaching entities: academic classroom instruction and clinical demonstrations and practice. As nurses recognized inadequacies in their training, nursing education continued in a state of flux, as attempts were made to devise the right combination of academic and clinical training.

Today, nursing continues to expand and continues to specialize. Thus, the educational needs of tomorrow's nurses will be quite different from what they are today. The key to the success of nursing has been, and will continue to be, its flexibility.

The nurse preceptor teaching programs operating in various areas today offer unique learning experiences that utilize innovative teacher-student relationships. For students with enough initiative to take responsibility for creating and directing their own learning experiences and career preparation, the opportunities are limitless.

---

**SUGGESTED READING**

Schweer, J. *Creative teaching in clinical nursing.* St. Louis, Mo.: C.V. Mosby Co., 1968.

# Chapter 15

# How To Work away from Campus under the Direction of a Preceptor

*Sue Thomas*

Some persons thrive on change, others do not, but almost everyone feels some discomfort when change occurs. Although the student who wants to work away from campus under the direction of a preceptor probably welcomes the challenge of new experiences, advance preparation can help to reduce the normal anxiety of change. The student can prepare for the experience psychologically by exploring personal and professional goals and identifying expectations of the preceptorship experience.

## THE STUDENT'S ROLE

In sorting out these expectations, the student will be reminded that projects and assignments in a preceptorship are experiential and individualized, while those on campus are usually general and given to all students. The campus assignments are graded, providing definite, objective feedback concerning the quality of the student's work. Even in clinical work on campus, immediate feedback and fairly close supervision are available. Feedback in a preceptorship does not come that neatly or consistently.

Supervision in a preceptorship is also different. One of the preceptor's objectives is to increase the student's professional autonomy; therefore the student is encouraged to be self-directed. To a great extent, the student determines the quality and quantity of the requirements.

Another aspect of preparation is analysis of what the student wants to gain from the experience away from campus. Self-exploration can lead to more specific objectives and the impetus to attain them. The goals need not be just professional. This is a particularly good time to consider personal goals and ways to integrate personal and professional goals. Themes of independence, adventure, and competence can be explored. Areas involving finances, relationships with others and with the natural world, and

127

one's spiritual, emotional and physical development are also worth investigating.

## THE PRECEPTOR'S ROLE

In general, a preceptor is concerned enough about nursing as a profession to help its students. Usually the preceptor is busy but wants to share experiences and knowledge in order to develop a student's abilities and confidence. The preceptor also shares clients. The willingness to trust a student with the preceptor's clients is balanced by the preceptor's responsibility to direct the student's learning experience.

Directing the student involves the planning and arranging of assignments, projects, and activities that will fulfill the student's learning objectives. The preceptor orients the student to the facility and its personnel policies, introduces the student to the staff, and helps the student feel like an accepted staff member. The preceptor supervises the student's clinical experience or arranges for a preceptor of comparable expertise to supervise the student in another facility. The preceptor encourages initiative, individuality, self-expression, and self-evaluation in the student. The supervision should decrease as the autonomy of the student is developed. Because of the preceptor's expertise and knowledge, the preceptor will serve as a resource for the student or may refer the student to other reliable sources. If skills are needed, the preceptor can either demonstrate the specific procedures or, again, recommend someone else who is qualified to do so.

## THE STUDENT-PRECEPTOR RELATIONSHIP

Early in the placement experience, the preceptor will propose those activities and projects that are likely to fulfill the student's learning objectives. These proposals are based on what is possible in the facility and area in the light of the student's learning objectives received prior to the student's arrival. Careful development of objectives will now be rewarded. If they have not already been identified, the student's hierarchical preferences can now be indicated. Together, the preceptor and student can discuss each other's expectations and work out a tentative schedule.

It is possible that the student has overlooked in the projected objectives a learning experience that is readily available in the placement locale. If open to experiences other than those already indicated, the student can communicate this fact to the preceptor. Initially, the establishment of open communication between the preceptor and student is vital. This commu-

nication is then facilitated by attitudes of flexibility, objectivity, cooperation, and tact.

The objectives and the activities planned for their implementation should
be reevaluated periodically to determine their usefulness and the progress
being made. If a project or activity is not satisfying or valuable to the
student, the student may wish to negotiate a change. Optimum use of the
student's time and abilities must remain a high priority for both student
and preceptor throughout the placement. A wise procedure is to schedule
weekly conferences, even if there is daily contact. A well-planned agenda
will be the student's responsibility. The preceptor may feel that this is an
area in which the student can develop initiative, organizational ability, and
assertiveness.

The weekly conference serves many functions. If feedback on the student's performance is not received, it can be forthrightly sought in such a
meeting. The conference is a time to identify problems in the work assignment, with other staff, or in the relationship between preceptor and
student. Problems can thus be managed as they arise. The professional
nurture available from the preceptor may be requested and, if given, should
be accepted gracefully.

The preceptor and student may not always be in accord. Disagreements
may occur over what constitutes valid work assignments, objectives, or
expectations. Discussion can be initiated by the student, preferably with
tact. If the student has acceptable alternatives to propose, viable compromises are likely to be worked out. Ideas for projects may come from facility
staff, other students in the placement program, the faculty coordinator, or
from the student's own increasing knowledge of the health concerns in the
community.

Conferences between the student and preceptor provide an excellent
opportunity to develop the communication skills and problem-solving abilities that will be essential in later relations with professional coworkers.
Conflicts will probably be minimal during the preceptorship, but they can
still provide excellent learning experiences. In rare cases, conflicts may
arise that prove overwhelming to the preceptor and student. If attempts
to reconcile such conflicts fail, it may be necessary to request assistance
from the faculty coordinator.

## THE LEARNING EXPERIENCE

As important as the relationship with the preceptor is to the student,
clinical assignments and selected projects constitute much of the learning
process. Here academic knowledge can be utilized and skills can be learned

and practiced. The student will be able to explore those facets of the profession the student is most interested in or, on the other hand, feels weakest in. The student should strive for a balanced program.

Since the student has, by means of stipulated objectives, created a personal design for the learning experience, the student will need to review and possibly modify the objectives frequently. Even though they may have been excellent objectives to begin with, some may need to be altered or deleted as the student adapts them to the placement assignment. Inventiveness in finding the means to meet the objectives and flexibility in the utilization of available experiences allows the student to exercise creativity and to gain confidence in the requisite abilities to achieve established goals.

Whatever the choice in using available time, the student has a rare opportunity to be "professional" before actually achieving that status. The student has the opportunity to interact on a professional basis not only with the preceptor but also with other staff in the facility. Prior to this time, the student has not worked closely for an extensive period of time with health professionals who are not part of the academic setting. It is important for the student to see how these people manage the stress of the profession, how they relate to each other as professionals, what their attitudes are toward work and their clientele, how, or if, they participate in community affairs, and how they integrate their personal and professional lives. However, instructive and enlightening as these observations of various practitioners are, the student need neither imitate nor reject the role models. Rather, the student can begin to evolve a style that reflects the student's own perspective and objectives.

An additional learning potential in placement away from campus includes the periodic meetings with other students who are working within meeting distance. Some students may have similar placements and work, but there will always be differences to explore as projects are presented and experiences shared. Best of all, other students can provide peer friendships that may not be available in the placement assignment. Recreational or professional activities may then be planned together. The students can also avail themselves of the coordinator, acting as facilitator and communicator.

The requirements imposed by the faculty coordinator can aid in this process. Of particular importance here is the requirement to maintain a log or journal as a personal and professional record of the student's life away from campus. The daily log provides a wonderful tool to evaluate the student's work and relationships and the quality of the student's experience. Reference to the journal after the placement assignment is finished is an excellent way to recall the total experience.

## POSITIVE BENEFITS

While students may feel that they are mostly the recipient of benefits in their placements away from campus, they also bring certain benefits with them. One quality that students often have, and health professionals some-times lose, is enthusiasm. Enthusiasm can spark a like response in the staff or clients the students work with. Health professionals need to have their optimism rekindled. Having an enthusiastic student around may prompt the staff to enliven their teaching, to brush up on some little-used skills, and even to reevaluate their own objectives. Undoubtedly, such students bring fresh perspectives to many of the clients they work with and, through the clients, to the staff with whom the students normally work.

As the students progress in their professional autonomy, they can relieve some of the workload of the preceptor. They can accomplish some projects the preceptor has meant to do but has not had time for. One of the most valuable gifts they can bring to those they work with is the mental stim-ulation of those whose minds are active because they are engaged in the learning process.

Mutual gratitude is often the natural outcome for both the student and preceptor. The student has brought to the precepting experience hopes, skills, energy, and a desire to learn. By the time of departure, if all goes well, the student will have gained a tremendous amount, not only in a professional sense, but also in the realm of personal growth and achievement.

# Chapter 16

# How To Gain Maximum Advantage from the Preceptor Clinical Experience

*Wendy Votroubek*

The role transition from student to professional is the major problem the nurse will face after graduation. Traditional clinical nursing does not lend itself to developing a strong sense of independence, self-responsibility, assertion of one's needs, and preparation in dealing with other members of the health team.

## THE REFINING PROCESS

In the latter part of training, after basic nursing skills have been learned, refinement is necessary to choose a specialty and to make a decision about where one will fit into the continuum of nursing. In this context, an assignment with a preceptor should be seen as an option, to help alleviate the reality shock.

Maralda (1977) has noted that "the growing emphasis of preceptors is born of a national concern over the current shortage of primary health care professionals and public pressure to increase the supply" (p. 69). The student internship provides the student a hands-on experience. It is also a chance to work more closely with a professional in the specialty of one's choice, an opportunity not often available through the traditional rotations in nursing school. Maralda concludes:

> By participating in this individual based learning experience, several advantages are recognized: development of clinical and professional competence in the delivery of nursing care; familiarity with the cultural, economic, political and environmental determinants of health in the particular community; learning the administrative and organizational structure of the local delivery system; and appreciation of the community's health needs as well

as career challenges and opportunities for nurses in the under-served areas (p. 69).

The preceptor experience also provides an opportunity to develop resourcefulness and assertive behavior. The students are involved in an independent setting away from the confines of a scheduled environment. They learn to depend on themselves for job satisfaction and finding new experiences. Individual interactions take place that facilitate the development of open, honest communication with the preceptor. What evolves is an opportunity to develop assertive thought, a chance to realize the skills to control one's behavior.

Bloom, Coburn, and Pearlman (1975) note that "assertive behavior can be described as those actions which demonstrate the intent to communicate honestly and directly, to make choices for oneself without harming or being harmed. On the other hand, nonassertive behavior is being indirect, inhibited, and self-denying, avoiding most of all unpleasant situations" (pp. 16–17). When working with a preceptor, the assertive student can help to alleviate or minimize problems that may occur. Assertive behavior can enable the student to utilize available resources, to be adaptable in the setting, and to ease the transition to a later career as a professional member of the health team. What is needed is to "state goals, identify limits, realize what you would like from others" (Bloom et al., 1975, pp. 16–17) and to take charge of your own behavior and be responsible for its outcomes. "By taking charge, developing the ability to find and mobilize resources, and realizing the only behavior that can be controlled is your own" (Burton & Wilson, 1977, p. 11), the student can facilitate a productive and reality-oriented experience.

## NEED FOR ASSERTIVENESS

Despite the increasing numbers of men joining the nursing profession, the fact remains that it is female-dominated, with a predetermined script. Women's socialization conditions them to a "woman's place": passive, submissive, dominated by men. "Part of the feminine ideal, the ability to please, is usually looked upon as a virtue, especially by men" (Grissum, 1976, p. 89). No real opportunities are given for determining her own position. On the contrary, women are seen as "risk takers and role breakers" (Grissum, 1976, p. 89) if they decide to plot their own course away from the traditional female orientation. The men in power expect women and other subordinates to please them and to support the status quo.

Thus, the traditional nurse's path from the institution of school to work does not necessarily lead to independence or a sense of autonomy among many skilled professionals. What usually results is reality shock; that is, one is expected to make the transition of being answerable to one's self, while at the same time remaining under the auspices of someone else's control. A sense of responsibility for individual actions or the ability of quality decision making are skills that are left for one to develop as a member of the health team.

Finding oneself caught between a prescribed role and a personal belief is a common manifestation of the reality of the health team. It may be explained further by a statement made by Grissum in 1960:

> The nurse serves almost as mother, almost as manager, and almost as healer. She navigates between allegiance to the hospital, to the physician and to the patient. She has responsibilities without formal sanctions and represents many symbols without filling any. This profession in its broad and multiple roles can be called the occupation of the not quite. (Grissum, 1976, p. 95)

Nurses must learn to survive in this profession and to succeed in today's world while defining their occupation. With intervention, it is possible to be recognized as a professional individual, not merely the handmaiden of the doctor. It is necessary to accept responsibility and accountability and to assume a self-concept that permits growth.

The feasibility of this occurring without conscious effort and intervention is minimal. The experience of working with the preceptor provides an opportunity for individual action to achieve self-satisfaction and actualization. The preceptor experience allows the student to choose those skills the student wants refined and to make critical decisions and accept responsibility for them. It is a chance to develop independence in the domain of nursing, without the geographical closeness to and dependence on a professor. It can also be a time of evaluation, of asserting one's self to fulfill the needs of nursing, something that is not always possible when doing clinical work in the college setting.

## OBJECTIVES FOR PERSONAL AND PROFESSIONAL GROWTH

Work with a preceptor provides an opportunity for freedom and professional and personal growth. However, it can also be a devastating experience for the student who is not prepared to cope without a close and familiar support system. Being with a preceptor involves taking risks to control one's own actions, within the limits of behavioral objectives. It is a time to identify priorities and goals and to become immersed in the professional role.

The student's goals become guidelines in formulating behavioral objectives for the precepting experience. These objectives assist the student in directing the learning experience. In writing objectives, it is imperative to have clearly identified expectations and to specify actions to achieve them. It is helpful to talk with the preceptor and faculty advisor while writing the objectives, but this is a personal decision, influenced by individual attitudes.

The student's objectives need to be specific, thereby lessening the chance of ambiguities. For example, for an objective to compare and contrast the role of public health nurse in a rural community with that of a public health nurse in Los Angeles County, a student might include the following specifics:

- Make at least three home visits per week to assess thoroughly the health needs of the families in the communities.
- Compare the rural community's need for health care to that of Los Angeles County.
- Attend a minimum of one prenatal clinic, ambulatory clinic, family planning clinic, or venereal disease clinic in each area and observe the duties of the public health nurse.
- Spend at least one day with the public health nurse from a home health agency.

It is advisable to work with the preceptor in revising the objectives, either before, during, or at the completion of the placement, depending on the situation. If the student and preceptor initiated communication prior to the placement, the revisions can hopefully be kept to a minimum. For those students who did not make contact with the preceptor before the rotation began, it is advisable to make these adjustments before too much time has elapsed, but not until the student has had a chance to appraise the situation and the initial shock of the placement has worn off.

To ensure that the objectives will be fulfilled, priorities are determined by the student and preceptor. This will also be done before the assignment or early in the rotation. After the preceptor experience has begun, those objectives that are specific to the preceptor's area of expertise may gain increasing significance. The essential element in the success of a preceptor is the willingness and ability of the student to maintain ultimate control and responsibility for fulfilling the student's clinical objectives.

Periodic conferences and evaluations with the preceptor are necessary to manage effectively the revisions in clinical objectives. In addition to discussing modifications of objectives, the student and preceptor can assess the progress made and discuss priorities for the remaining weeks. Ideally, the periodic evaluations should be utilized to appraise not only the student's status but also the dynamics of the student's relationship with the preceptor. This will demonstrate the effectiveness of working together and again permit changes to be made.

## BENEFITS OF STUDENT-PRECEPTOR INTERACTION

During the revisions, priority settings, or evaluations, the student and preceptor may not agree. This may create misunderstandings or hard feelings between the two. However, based on the preceptor's previous experience with the student, to make the relationship a productive one and not a means of coercion, it is important to think of it, not as a confrontation, but rather as a means of sharing expectations, goals, feelings, and opinions.

An additional factor that could make the rotation easier for the student is the acquisition of information on a specific area of health care, especially if the student is unfamiliar with that area specialty. If it is possible to have contact with the preceptor before the rotation starts, the student can research certain books and periodicals to increase the student's knowledge base. Also it is helpful to become familiar with the personal philosophy of the preceptor. This is usually done after the student has begun the assignment, but it would also be advantageous to discuss philosophies prior to the rotation, if possible. By doing such basic groundwork, the student is able to increase the opportunities for specific learning, instead of spending time only with basic research.

The student's relationship with a preceptor is not meant to be one in which the student receives all the benefits. On the contrary, the student's determination to achieve goals should involve the preceptor in a mutual exchange of benefits. Ways for the student to share knowledge and energy with the preceptor might include teaching a project for a specific population of clients, assisting in updating referrals or protocols, taping information about a health problem, or annotating a bibliography to supplement the general information base of the agency.

**REFERENCES**

Bloom, L.Z.; Coburn, K.; & Pearlman, J. *The new assertive woman.* New York: Dell, 1975.

Burton, P., & Wilson, H.S. The death of Sue Barton. *Occupational Health Nursing,* August 1977, 110.

Grissum, M. How to become a risk taker and a role maker. *Nursing 76,* November 1976, 89, 95.

Maralda, P.J. Better nursing care through preceptorships. *RN,* March 1977, 69.

# Chapter 17

# The Rewards of a Preceptor Clinical Assignment—A Personal Experience

*Katherine Jensen*

There are nine patients on the floor, more than half of our total capacity.

There are two new mothers in the room at the end of the hall. Their babies sleep contentedly in bed beside them. They've been instructed on how to use the bulb syringe (please, don't let them need it); but otherwise, they're on their own this shift.

The cardiac monitor beats endlessly on the shelf above my head. Across the hall, an 87-year-old man sleeps fitfully, artifact reflecting every toss and turn. His wife of 60 years sits quietly beside his bed. Sinus tachycardia, occasional multifocal PVCs (please, don't code). We watch him through the night, waiting on enzymes, ruling out MI.

The whir of the mist tent is a constant drone from pediatrics. We have a nine month old with croup. The trach tray is in the room (please, little one, keep breathing).

There are three medical patients occupying the rooms between OB and pediatrics. One has cellulitis, two have pneumonia, all three have IVs (please, don't let them infiltrate, please let them run on time). All three patients have IV piggybacks that must be mixed and hung on time.

The emergency room bell has rung every 30 minutes since I came on. There have been no real emergencies (thank God), no life and death decisions. I've had to call the doctor in a dozen times. I'm running out of suture trays and size-eight gloves. I've given endless meds for pain.

My aide stays on the floor to answer lights and watch the monitor when I must be in ER. I'm the only RN on duty. It's the P.M. shift; the hospital belongs to us.

Two evenings later, there are no patients. Everyone has gone home or been transferred. The ER bell doesn't ring during the entire shift. We make up charts, put away linens, clean cupboards, read policy manuals, occupy the time.

Rural nursing! Was I prepared for this? Yes, but not from anything I learned inside a classroom.

A graduate of a progressive and well-respected ADN program, I trained in a community that I considered "rural." There were three hospitals in town. The largest had a capacity of 120 beds; there were usually 60 to 80 patients in the house. I worked medical floor OR, surgical floor OR, a specialty area—*one* department at a time. We did team leading and total patient care. We were seldom out of things. Central Supply magically appeared at 3 P.M. and filled our carts. Pharmacy came twice a day and filled my med cart with exactly what I needed to get me through my shift; the IVPBs were always mixed and waiting in the refrigerator.

There was always someone around to start the IV if I couldn't get it in—a charge nurse, my supervisor, or the nurse anesthetist who could start an IV in a two-pound preemie with one hand tied behind his back. Exaggerated, but reassuring; he was a phone call away.

There were teams who did nothing but change IV tubing. The ICU/CCU/ER nurses served as our code team. The kitchen left complete meals that could be warmed in the microwave for the few hours that they were off duty. Housekeeping cleaned the rooms as fast as we moved the patients out; any spills or extra work, and we could have them paged. There was respiratory therapy that kept the halls resounding with clapping and percussion and coughing; physical therapy, walking patients up and down the corridors; patient teaching teams. Oxygen, compressed air, and suction came from holes and dials that were mounted on the walls beside each bed.

Now, all departments occupy a single hall. I am nursing (charge, supervisor, and staff), pharmacy, RT, PT, ward clerk, and Addressograph. Often, I am central supply, dietary, housekeeping, and maintenance. After a late delivery, I'm in the kitchen trying to put together a reasonably attractive dinner for a ravenous new mother.

Unit dose does not exist up here. I measure out and mix my meds. There is no backup, except the doctor who is "on the way." If I don't get the IV in, the patient could die. Equipment is from another age. Oxygen comes in green tanks, compressed air in pink. Suction is the machine we haul out of the closet when we need it.

I had been out of school less than four months when I took this job. I worked eight weeks as an interim permittee in one of the hospitals that I had trained in and then packed up husband and two children and moved 600 miles away from friends and family to work in a 16-bed hospital in the mountains of northern California. It is the only facility serving an area of approximately 150 square miles.

I knew that this was the kind of nursing I wanted to do. I knew that I could do it. That came, not from the arrogance of the new grad who believes she can do anything, but from true awareness. As a student enrolled in the Rural Clinical Nurse Placement Program and given a preceptor assignment, I had the experience of rural nursing to support my decision to choose rural nursing. I have never suffered from "reality shock."

There is no way to discover what rural nursing is without experiencing it. I have repeatedly run into two reactions to written and verbal descriptions. Either it's seen as "romantic," and there is great desire to move to the woods for some grand adventure; or there is tremendous apprehension and fear of responsibility and risk to licensure for performing expected duties that may be questionable in the light of the standards of nursing practice. And then there are the nurses who come to the rural hospital, either with the "romantic" ideal in mind or with the expectation of finding a "real" hospital. They then quickly become angry at the realities: the unpredictability of working conditions, the overwork or underwork, the understaffing or overstaffing, the amount of responsibility, the underpay for important responsibilities, and the repeated "unusual" or "special" situations that make it impossible to apply the training and methodology that are taught in city schools.

I can hardly remember what a Swanns-Gann catheter looks like. I went a year without exposure to a CVP line and a year and a half without seeing a colostomy. (Whatever happened to "ostomy teams" and the extensive patient teaching programs that I left in town?) This is a rural community, a logging area with rugged mountain roads. We see trauma here, and lots of injuries, accidental and otherwise. Nursing is different here. I am gaining new skills and losing old ones. But I know that this is the kind of nursing that I want to do, and I make the trade-offs willingly.

When I enrolled in the preceptor program, I'd never been in a hospital smaller than the ones I'd trained in. I considered such a hospital "rural." I was assigned to a 25-bed facility in a mountainous community similar to the one where I now make my home. I walked into the hospital and found myself confronted with narrow, uncarpeted, poorly lit hallways that were lined with wheelchairs, gurneys, and other equipment that was not in use.

Greeted enthusiastically by the staff where I had trained, I now found myself viewed with suspicion. I was an outsider, an oddity. They had never seen a student nurse at this hospital. The nurse on duty had been there for 25 years; she still stood when the doctors entered the nurse's station. She followed the doctors during rounds, holding charts. The doctors told me to "pay attention," she's an example of an "excellent" nurse. They had never worked with most of the equipment that I took for granted. I had never worked where oxygen didn't come out of the wall.

We stared at each other like inhabitants of different planets. I had come expecting a teaching-learning environment, a staff who would willingly teach me how to adapt my newly acquired nursing skills to the rural setting. They received me, expecting judgment, the pointing out of shortcomings, the arrogance of the new grad who "knows everything." Neither of us had our expectations met.

I could spend four weeks trying to convince these people to teach me the things that I had come to learn, or I could choose silence and learn from observation. I chose the latter. I learned to bend. I made friends with adaptability and flexibility, and the personal gain from the acquisition of those skills was immeasurable.

The doctors were right; she was an "excellent" nurse, though not for the reasons they implied. She knew nothing about "nursing diagnosis" or circoelectric beds or cardiac monitors, but her nursing skills were timeless and she had lots to teach.

The differences in nursing are innumerable, but it is not in the recognition of those differences that the greatest personal gain from the preceptor experience lies.

A rural community is a unique place to live. I am 53 miles from the closest town of any size, 53 miles over roads that are treacherous in winter and responsible for countless motor vehicle accidents throughout the year. I don't go to town very often. I can't go to the store and take for granted that I will find the merchandise I need. Supplies are limited and not matched to my life style. I am no longer in a college community and, philosophically, no longer in the mainstream. My neighbors have been here for generations, for thousands of years. The same families have been in power for as long as anyone can remember. As a white, middle-class, college-educated American, I am, for the first time, a minority.

My preceptor assignment not only confronted me with the realities of rural nursing, but with the realities of rural living; the two are very closely connected. The greatest personal gain from the assignment was the experience it gave me in dealing with people whose life style and philosophy were different from my own.

There is a saying that the best way to learn a foreign language is to live in the country whose language you are trying to learn. The need to communicate will be sufficient motivation, and the language will be learned quickly and well. The same is true of rural nursing and rural living. A preceptor assignment provides the ticket to the foreign country and an extraordinary learning experience.

In traditional nurse training programs, you go to your clinical assignment, do your work, and then go home. Exposure to different cultures and different life styles is limited to classroom lectures, the time spent in clinical work, and the differences available in the fairly homogenous communities in which nursing schools are located. With a preceptor assignment, each hour of the day is "clinical." The training is not just in nursing, but in living.

I learned a lot about nursing, about small towns and small-town politics, about the people who choose to live their lives in a rural community. But those are just the obvious gains in growing. The experience offered a lot more to me. I had never lived away from home, never lived away from friends or family, never driven more than 40 miles away from home. A preceptor assignment can be a "half-way house" for those students who have never really lived on their own before. The program provides housing and a clinical assignment. The student creates the experience. The opportunity for that kind of "safe" independence does not come often.

I had always had things done for me. I went to classes at scheduled times, completed assignments according to due dates. In a preceptor assignment, there is no one else planning the program. Where the preceptor is involved and enthusiastic about teaching, there is added guidance, but that was not true in my case. My preceptor was overwhelmed with other responsibilities, and I was on my own. The independence was good for me. I created my own experience. I explored rural nursing and rural living and was able to get a feel for what it was all about. By the time I left, I had *earned* the respect that I had expected to be *given* me when I arrived. The success of that experience is immeasurable in terms of gain to self-confidence and self-esteem.

I spent several years listening to nurses and nursing instructors recommend at least a year in med-surg before moving into a specialty area. It is important, they said, to gain the experience necessary to really learn the skills you are exposed to in nursing school, to build the confidence to act independently and yet still function as a member of a team. I think about that message every time I have a patient on the monitor and realize that I do not work with it often enough to feel truly confident. But my preceptor assignment made me aware that there are other options, or at least supplements, to a year in med-surg.

A preceptor assignment teaches independence, while making it very apparent that nursing is a team effort. In a rural community, you can't function effectively without the support of the team. You learn skills that you cannot learn elsewhere, and you gain confidence that will benefit any nurse in any field of nursing.

I gained independence, self-confidence, rural nursing skills, adaptability, flexibility, awareness, and invaluable experience in living. We are all individuals, with individual needs. We all grow in our own way. A preceptor assignment is a uniquely personal experience. For the student who is truly open to learning, it shapes itself to meet that student's needs. The student is the creator and not the created. The gain in personal growth, as well as in nursing skills, is invaluable. It's an exciting and challenging experience where what you gain is truly dependent on what you have to give. It's your experience, and it cannot be gained in the classroom.

---

**SUGGESTED READINGS**

Kozier, B., & Erb, G.L. *Fundamentals of nursing.* Menlo Park, Calif.: Addison-Wesley Publishing Co., 1979.

Kramer, M., & Schmalenberg, C. *Reality shock.* St. Louis, Mo.: C.V. Mosby Co., 1974.

Wilson, H.S., & Kneisl, C.R. *Psychiatric nursing.* Menlo Park, Calif.: Addison-Wesley Publishing Co., 1979.

# Part IV

# Having Students in Your Facility—The Administrator's Perspective

# Chapter 18

# Legal Considerations for the Nursing Service Administrator Involved with a Clinical Preceptor Contract

*Frank T. Farnkopf*

In initiating a student preceptor clinical contract, a nursing service administrator must consider the legal ramifications of the nursing student working in the clinical setting. The nursing service administrator may choose to address this issue directly at the beginning of the contract formulation or defer investigation to another "more appropriate" time. However, there will probably be other members of the agency who will feel inclined to address the issue immediately. These people may be the chief executive officer, various members of the nursing and medical staffs, and probably the student and the preceptor. In any event, since the student and preceptor are directly involved with the nursing service, it is probably appropriate for the nursing service administrator to discuss policy with them and answer their questions.

## THE STUDENT'S LEGAL STATUS

Unfortunately the legal ramifications of a student-preceptor clinical arrangement are not clearly addressed in the literature presently available. Obviously, the student with a license must practice within the limits of the nurse practice act of the student's state. The student is held accountable for all actions based upon the state's nurse practice act and for all the obligations regarding client litigation that may ensue. For example, the student must be under the supervision of the preceptor (or a designated substitute preceptor in the temporary absence of the preceptor) at all times. The preceptor must be licensed and must be thoroughly oriented to the agency and its nursing care units, policies, and procedures. In this way, the preceptor may be held accountable for providing safe preceptorship experiences and close supervision of the student. To utilize a preceptor who cannot be held totally accountable for all actions of the student in a clinical setting is an act of negligence by the preceptor, the nursing service administrator, and the health care agency providing the clinical setting.

With respect to a student possessing a valid license, that is, a student nurse working on a BSN who is already licensed, it is the responsibility of the nursing service administrator to determine the nursing skills and abilities of each student regardless of whether the student is presently licensed. This is simply a matter of preventing malpractice on a client by a student who may not have sufficient skills or knowledge to practice safely in the clinical setting. This situation may arise in the case of the newly licensed nursing student who has not had sufficient time and experience to acquire an all-around proficiency. As we all know, what we learn in school never completely prepares us for what we encounter in the real world of nursing. Fortunately we can learn through experience while practicing.

State boards of nursing licensure test for the minimal technical and theoretical nursing abilities that are acceptable for the professional practice of nursing at various levels of licensure (for example, the licensed vocational nurse or registered nurse). For this reason, it is important to evaluate immediately the new nursing student to determine the student's skill and theory level relative to the type of nursing care to be delivered.

## CLOSE STUDENT SUPERVISION

Legally, the importance of thoroughly evaluating and testing the student's knowledge in a new clinical setting cannot be overemphasized. The agency is responsible to its clients to minimize (if not prevent) errors or accidents in procedural nursing care that the student might deliver. It is very easy for persons who are new to a nursing unit to make errors during orientation that they would not normally make once they are thoroughly oriented to and comfortable in the patient care setting. For this reason, it is critical that the student be very closely supervised and monitored in all aspects of care by the preceptor. The nursing service administrator is responsible for ensuring that the student's clinical preceptors understand their responsibilities in the critical orientation period during which the student is observed for proficiency. To do less may constitute negligence and malpractice on the part of the preceptor and the nursing service administrator, who is ultimately accountable for the care delivered in the clinical care units and the nursing service as a whole.

## ELEMENTS OF THE PRECEPTORSHIP CONTRACT

For all students who participate with the health care agency in a student-preceptor clinical experience, a representative of the student's academic institution must sign a contract involving all parties of the preceptor program.

*First*, when the educational institution begins the selection process of the appropriately qualified student, it will provide a nursing faculty member to initiate negotiations between the student and the health care agency. The school will also monitor the progress of the student throughout the clinical placement in light of the student's approved goals and objectives in the student-preceptor clinical arrangement. It is very important for all parties involved in the student-preceptor situation that communication patterns be firmly established between all entities responsible for the student's welfare (including the university and the health care agency). Communication channels must be open throughout the student placement. Even after the placement is over, the facilitation of constructive feedback is necessary to ensure continuing effective coordination between all parties involved. All information received from exit interviews should be relayed promptly from the university to the appropriate parties in the health care agency. This will help the health care agency to eliminate deficits and reinforce positive aspects of the experience.

*Second*, the health care agency must designate appropriate clinical staff and provide appropriate clinical experiences necessary to meet the learning objectives of the student. These must include a clinical setting that is harmonious for the student, the client, and the staff. The student must be thoroughly oriented to the facility and its goals and objectives for delivering health care to the community it serves. The preceptor of the student must be available to the student at all times when in the clinical setting. The health care agency should be prepared to provide emergency health care to the student (with any financial liabilities assumed by the student) in case of clinical injury. However, the health care agency should not financially compensate the student for clinical time spent for academic credit. While in the clinical setting, accomplishing academic goals and objectives, the student should not for any reason be considered part of the employed workforce of the health care agency and should not be expected to function in this capacity for the health care agency. The health care agency should have the authority to consult with the educational institution and any other sponsoring agency. If, in the opinion of the health care agency, the student in a student-preceptor contractual relationship either (1) is not meeting the specified goals and objectives for clinical placement and participation or (2) is not appropriately trained to participate safely with the clients, the health care agency, after consultation with all involved parties, should have the right to discharge the student. The health care agency must at all times protect the rights of the clients who are exposed to students in the agency.

Whenever appropriate, the health care agency is expected to be able to describe and discuss the student's level of proficiency.

*Third*, all parties involved in a student-preceptor arrangement should be held accountable for not violating individual rights, for example, by discriminating on the basis of age, sex, or national origin.

*Fourth*, there should be specific beginning and ending dates of placement for each student preceptorship.

*Fifth*, there should be a specific clause in the contract relieving all the parties involved of all financial responsibilities and obligations. This includes payments from state programs such as state workman's compensation.

*Sixth*, upon mutual agreement, all parties involved should have the option to modify in writing any terms of the agreement at any time.

*Seventh*, the contract should be signed by two representatives of each party involved in the agreement: the educational institution, the health care agency, and any other sponsoring agency. The signature of the student is not needed since the student's participation in the program is sanctioned by the academic institution, which is considered ultimately responsible for the student's participation in the student-preceptor contract.

As in all contracts, the language should be simple and should address the specific needs of the sponsoring parties involved in the student-preceptor arrangement. The contract should be designed for the protection of each party involved. The obligations of each participant should be clearly specified. A typical student-preceptor letter of agreement is presented as Exhibit 18–1.

## CONFIDENTIALITY

The issue of confidentiality in patient care is especially important in the clinical health care setting. In the larger urban health care setting, confidentiality may not be so crucial, since most clients there are from a large population and thus tend to be more anonymous, both as they enter the health care system and as they leave to return to their separate lives. In the nonurban health care setting, however, where there is less anonymity, confidentiality should be a matter of particular concern to all members of the health care agency involved with patient care. Unfortunately, students who are exposed to smaller health care systems often do not have a good understanding of the importance of patient confidentiality. They may not be sufficiently sensitive to the need to protect the client's confidentiality. Thus, in such a setting, it is very important to emphasize to the student the problems involved with patient confidentiality and the profound impact a careless statement can have upon a client.

**Exhibit 18–1** Preceptorship Contract

*LETTER OF AGREEMENT*

The _____ , the Rural Clinical Nurse Placement Center—
Educational Institution

California State University, Chico, and _____ hereinafter
Health Agency/Individual

referred to as the health agency, agree to the following responsibilities related to students
enrolled in _____ who are participating in the Rural Clinical Nurse
Educational Institution

Placement Center and receiving field instruction in the above agency.

I. The Educational Institution shall:
   A. Select educationally prepared students for this rural clinical placement experience.
   B. Provide for a nursing faculty member to collaborate with the health agency clinical preceptor and Rural Clinical Nurse Placement nursing staff.
   C. Approve the student's learning objectives which will then be sent to the RCNPC and the Clinical Preceptor.
   D. Determine the units of academic credit to be granted to the student who successfully completes this clinical option.
   E. Provide an evaluation form for the student and clinical preceptor to complete at the conclusion of the student's experience.
   F. Submit an evaluation of the student's learning experience to the Rural Clinical Nurse Placement Center upon completion of that experience.

II. Rural Clinical Nurse Placement Center—California State University, Chico shall:
   A. Have nursing staff available at all times for consultation to students, faculty, and clinical preceptors.
   B. Make regular and requested visits to clinical placement sites where students are assigned.
   C. Provide the health agency with information about the student prior to his/her arrival.
   D. Notify the educational institution of the placement site and preceptor the student will be assigned to.
   E. Orient clinical preceptors to the placement program and their role as clinical preceptors as needed.
   F. Orient students to the program, the community, and the agency to which assigned as well as their responsibilities as participants in this placement program.
   G. Obtain documentation demonstrating that each student is covered by professional liability insurance.
   H. Will not assume financial responsibility for student while he/she is participating in this placement program.

III. The Health Agency shall:
   A. Provide each student with clinical experiences necessary to meet his/her learning objectives.
   B. Designate an appropriate staff member to act as the clinical preceptor who will assume responsibility for student supervision.
   C. Provide the resources needed for a desirable learning climate.
   D. Assure that staff is adequate in number and quality to insure safe and continuous health care to individuals.

## Exhibit 18–1 continued

E. Provide Rural Clinical Nurse Placement nursing staff and faculty access to the agency and agency staff.

F. Orient Center staff or faculty and students to the agency purposes, policies, and procedures.

G. Within its limited service capabilities provide emergency care for students in case of injury, with any financial liability assumed by the student for that service.

H. Shall not financially compensate any student receiving academic credit according to this Agreement nor shall students be considered employees of the health agency.

I. Have the right, after consultation with the Rural Clinical Nurse Placement Center and the educational institution to refuse to accept or continue any nursing student, who in the health agency's judgment, is not participating satisfactorily or safely in this placement.

J. Any problem reflecting on the qualifications of a student shall be immediately called to the attention of the Rural Clinical Nurse Placement Center and the educational institution.

K. Maintain standards accepted by appropriate accrediting bodies, as applicable.

L. Participate in written evaluations of the student's performance and of the Rural Clinical Nurse Placement Center.

IV. The parties of this Agreement shall not discriminate against any student because of age, sex, or national origin.

V. Financial responsibility:
By this Agreement none of the parties incur any responsibility for financial exchange whether in monies or in kind.

VI. Period of Agreement:
This Agreement shall be in effect beginning _____, 19_____ and shall remain in effect for one year from the date of Agreement or until terminated by one of the parties who shall provide three (3) months written notice of their decision. This Agreement automatically terminates upon the completion of the Rural Clinical Nurse Placement Center.

VII. This Agreement may at any time be altered, changed or amended by mutual agreement of the parties in writing.

IN WITNESS WHEREOF, this Agreement has been signed by and on behalf of the parties identified above.

For the Educational Institution:

By _____ Date _____
    Chairperson, Nursing Program

By _____ Date _____
    Representative of Educational Institution

For the Rural Clinical Nurse Placement Center:

By _____ Date _____
    Director

**Exhibit 18–1** continued

For the California State University, Chico:

By _____ Date _____
    Purchasing Officer

For the Health Agency:

By _____ Date _____
    Nursing Service Administrator

By _____ Date _____
    Agency Administrator or Physician

*Source:* Rural Clinical Nurse Placement Center, California State University, Chico. Used with permission.

Health care providers often lose touch with the closely knit community environment in which they practice and provide nursing care. Yet it is very important that health care providers be conscious of the importance of confidentiality in the interactions they have with their clients and with the community in which they work and live. The student does not have the time to develop this street-wise awareness of client confidentiality. Thus, it becomes the responsibility of the preceptor and others in the health care staff to raise the student's awareness of this issue as quickly as possible. It is the responsibility of the nursing service administrator to ensure that the student will be counseled accordingly. Otherwise, a client's rights to confidentiality may be compromised and the health care facility may find itself involved in justified litigation.

## ACCOUNTABILITY

The student who does not have a license in a particular area of nursing practice may also be a matter of concern. For example, a student may be currently enrolled in a nursing education program but not have taken the necessary licensure board examinations midway through the nursing program. In this situation, whatever clinical activities the student performs are done under the sanctions provided by the licensure of the preceptor. The preceptor will be held accountable for any harmful or potentially harmful actions that the student might perform upon a client. The preceptor of a nonlicensed student will be held accountable for the student's actions within the framework of the preceptor's license under the nursing practice act of the licensing state. The preceptor of a nonlicensed student is responsible for ensuring appropriate supervision, orientation, and practice.

In the case of the preceptor supervising a licensed student, the professional liability and responsibility of the preceptor apply primarily during orientation. After orientation, the student is accountable for professional performance under the student's own license.

## OTHER STAFF AND AGENCY CONCERNS

Once the nursing service administrator is comfortable with a student-preceptor clinical arrangement, the legal ramifications of the arrangement must be communicated to other important members of the health care agency's staff. Often the term *student* is anxiety-producing for members of the medical, nursing, ancillary, or administrative staff. If the students have their own professional licensure, the anxiety of the staff may be lessened. By carefully explaining that the student will be closely supervised at all times by an experienced staff member, anxiety levels can also be lowered dramatically. Finally, after the legal ramifications of a student-preceptor arrangement have been carefully considered and explained and the appropriate precautions have been taken, the concerns of various staff members are likely to be considerably alleviated. In any case, the nursing service administrator must thoroughly explore all of the legal aspects involved in a student placement to protect the client, the student, the preceptor, and, ultimately, the health care agency.

After exposure to various student nurse-preceptor clinical experiences, it will become apparent that, through orientation and understanding of the various legal considerations relating to the staff (and to a certain extent the clients), the liabilities can be minimized. Results from ongoing risk-management analysis systems indicate that, aside from the obvious licensure and supervision considerations, the actual care provided by students produces less risk than that provided by the employed house staff. Student documentation of patient care is usually more precise, more thorough, and more appropriate to the overall goals of the health care team. Students tend to be much more concerned with patient and staff safety. They also tend to be more objective about established (agency-specific) routines in patient care. They are often either more supportive or more critical of those routines in light of their sensitivity and objectivity. With thorough orientation, students become aware of the legal considerations regarding their placement in a facility and, as a result, act responsibly, keeping in mind the needs of their clients, their fellow staff, and the preceptor of the nursing service or health care agency.

At present, there appears to be no documentation of litigation pertaining to clinical situations involving student nurses and preceptors. This may be an indication that all potential legal liabilities are presently being carefully considered and monitored to minimize the risks involved in a preceptorship in a health care facility. In any event, it is very important that the nursing service administrator thoroughly understand and minimize potential risks. This can be done by thorough orientation of the involved student, preceptor, staff, and clients (when appropriate) and by consistent monitoring of staff and student compliance with the preceptorship's guidelines as they relate to student orientation, supervision, client confidentiality, quality patient care, and staff understanding and cooperation.

# Chapter 19

# Criteria for Evaluating a Clinical Setting for a Preceptorship

*Frank T. Farnkopf*

A number of variables must be considered in the evaluation of a clinical setting to be used for a student-preceptor training program. The variables include, but are not limited to, (1) the amount and variety of clinical experiences available to the student, (2) the staff and community acceptance of a student-preceptor arrangement, (3) alternate clinical learning situations available in-house and throughout the community, (4) the relative proximity of educational resource centers, (5) the availability of student housing, (6) social and recreational activities, and (7) transportation available to the student.

## STAFF AND PATIENT ACCEPTANCE

Most important to the ultimate success of the student in meeting specified goals and objectives is the accepting attitude of the clients and staff that the student will be exposed to during the assignment at the health care agency. For the most part, the client population will be very accepting of a student if the rest of the staff has already expressed a favorable and accepting attitude. Patients usually pick up on the negative feelings from staff and other patients. In any case, it is of paramount importance to eliminate any negative feelings experienced by either patients or staff before the student is exposed to the clinical setting.

Often a new face (whether it be a student or a new staff member) on a nursing unit is cause for alarm on the part of members of the nursing and ancillary staffs. New faces usually mean new or different ideas, which may mean change. This can be very threatening and disconcerting to established staff. Sometimes students are very outspoken about what they see in a new clinical setting. Their comments may be intended to be helpful, but may still be interpreted as intrusion by the staff. The staff then is immediately on the defensive, which further compounds the situation. Thus, it is important for the nursing service administrator to be aware of the sensitivities and insecurities of the student and staff and to support both parties appropriately as the need arises.

Often the assignment of a student to a specific staff member is viewed by other staff as a prestige assignment. This could result in the student and the preceptor receiving expressions of verbal or nonverbal hostility from rival staff members. It is important for the nursing service administrator to be aware of the insecurities of the staff and the overt or passive aggressive behavior that may result. The atmosphere and conditions in a unit shift constantly and need to be periodically reevaluated. In most situations, it is possible to smooth the ruffled feathers of those who feel slighted because they were not given the student-preceptor assignment. Sometimes it is necessary to reject a student assignment because of an unfavorable and unaccepting staff situation.

In any case, it is important for the student to be placed in a learning environment that is accepting, tolerant, understanding, considerate, and flexible to the needs of the student in the new and unfamiliar clinical setting. If necessary, it is the responsibility of the nursing administrator, by eliciting the support of the staff or student, to modify the environment in which the student is placed. This may include behavior modification or even, as a last resort, elimination of a student-preceptor assignment.

If the staff is not accepting of a student assignment, the clients will notice immediately. They will be uncomfortable, confused, and distrustful and may even avoid the student, which will further detract from the student's learning experience (if not totally negate it). The staff must be very supportive of the student in order to make the patients feel comfortable when interacting with the student. This means that the nursing service administrator must be very supportive of the nursing staff and express appreciation for their efforts to meet the emotional and clinical needs of the student. If this is not feasible, the nursing service administrator must make appropriate adjustments to either improve the situation or eliminate the assignment.

Other problems may arise with insecure or apprehensive medical staff who will be interacting with the student, the preceptor, and the client. As we have noted, it may be necessary for the nursing administrator to reevaluate the "climate" of the clinical setting with regard to acceptance and support of the student. It may be necessary to modify the environment with appropriate support to the other medical staff members. If the unaccepting behavior cannot be modified, it may not be appropriate to go ahead with the student-preceptor assignment at that time. Usually, however, with verbal support from the nursing service administrator, it is possible to create a favorable and accepting climate, thereby facilitating beneficial student staff interactions. Most nurses and physicians enjoy an opportunity to teach someone who is interested in learning about a clinical unit and the individuals responsible for making it operate effectively. Students usually thrive in this type of learning environment. Sometimes, all it takes for success is a little verbal support and encouragement of the preceptorship model by the nursing service administrator.

## TYPE OF CLINICAL EXPERIENCE

The second most important factor to consider is the amount and variety of clinical experience that the student will be exposed to in the preceptor assignment. It is very important to match carefully the student's goals and objectives with the services and census that the agency is capable of providing. On some types of nursing care units, it is not possible to predict accurately the types of learning situations the student can be exposed to during a given assignment period. Obviously, the longer the period of assignment, the more time that will be available to guarantee that the student will be exposed to a sufficient variety of learning situations to meet established student goals and objectives. To justify the student's placement, there must be effective utilization of time spent versus significant clinical exposure.

The seasonal census cycles and illness patterns that are common to all hospitals are other factors to consider in determining the amount and types of clinical learning situations as they relate to the student's goals and objectives. The seasonal illness patterns are usually more predictable than the seasonal census cycles. There are winter-associated illnesses and slow census patterns in the winter months. The problem of seasonality is often less significant in the larger health care center where there is a larger patient population to draw from for admissions. Also, in such centers, patients with a greater variety of illnesses are admitted. This is a critical factor in determining if it is practical to accept a student for the months of December, January, and February, when hospitals are historically operated with a lower census than throughout the remainder of the year.

During the winter months, there are ways to modify a clinical situation that is seasonally slow and somewhat undiversified in disease types. Depending on the student's goals and objectives, there are alternative learning situations that might include neighborhood health care clinics, individual physician offices, school nursing support services, visiting nurse agencies, public health agencies, industrial nursing support services, and so on. With some support and assistance by the nursing service administrator, the student can gain access to different community health care agencies for increased exposure in meeting goals and objectives. Usually, the various agencies are very cooperative. If necessary, a little public relations effort by the nursing service administrator will eliminate any reluctance or hesitancy by agencies that are approached to cooperate in providing clinical exposure for the student.

## COMMUNITY SUPPORT FACILITIES

Another factor to consider is the availability and proximity of educational resource centers for the student. This is particularly problematic in small urban hospitals or rural health care centers with limited medical library resources. Most students are familiar with large medical centers with extensively developed resource learning centers. Usually students in a student-preceptor assignment are required to continue formal out-of-classroom studies related to research topics and theses on specific health care issues or situations. However, most health care agencies do not have sophisticated learning resource centers readily available for the student.

However, it is important to have such academic support services available to the student within a short traveling distance on at least a weekly basis. It is important to remember that as the student is exposed to new clinical situations in the preceptor health care setting, the student will have new questions stemming from participation in the preceptorship relationship. It is necessary for the student to be able to research such questions in order to address appropriately the goals and objectives that have been formulated for the clinical preceptor experience. Travel of two or three hours to university libraries is not unreasonable on a weekly basis, even in light of the often severely limited financial resources available to the student during preceptor participation.

Community housing for students gaining experiences away from campus in a preceptorship is always a potential problem. It is important to provide the student with a housing situation that will maximize clinical coordination as well as quality exposure to community social life. The decision to participate in a clinical preceptor placement requires that the student leave an established and comfortable existence with established support systems, both clinically and socially. Acceptance of a preceptorship can result in a living situation with relatively few such support systems. It involves a considerable amount of risk taking for the student to go from a comfortable, established living situation to an unknown one.

Thus, it is necessary that the student be housed in a setting that will be supportive and not detract from or interfere with the benefits to be gained from the clinical preceptorship. Housing selection is a problem of course because there is usually not a plethora of low-cost, short-term housing available in either rural or urban areas. Of course, the ideal housing situation would be one that affords a wide and diverse exposure to community social and political structures. To this end, a nursing service administrator can actively research potential housing situations and discriminate as appropriate. Frequently, established hospital staff can provide appropriate housing for students on a short-term, low-cost basis.

The availability of recreational and social opportunities is another important aspect of student placement. Different life styles, different daily activities, and different recreational and social activities will be encountered during the preceptor assignment. This can require a difficult adjustment for the student, particularly when all other support systems have been removed temporarily. At this time, it may be helpful for the nursing service administrator to include the student in appropriate social and recreational activities of the preceptor health care agency. Urban recreational activities are not difficult to find; rural recreational facilities may be more difficult to locate. In any case, the student should have access to the social and recreational life styles of the health care professional in the preceptorship environment.

Transportation is also a concern of the nursing service administrator in evaluating a potential preceptor assignment. The student's access to transportation is crucial to effectively fulfilling the established goals and objectives of the preceptorship in the clinical setting. Often a student comes from an urban setting where transportation is relatively easy to find; there are usually alternative means available if the automobile fails. In many nonurban settings, on the other hand, alternative transportation systems are virtually nonexistent. Also, climatic conditions may be more extreme and less controllable or predictable. Distances to essential services are longer, and fewer support services are available when automobiles break down. Given these uncertainties, it is important for the nursing service administrator to help the student understand and contend with the transportation factors that might impede or make unsafe the student's participation in clinical activities. No matter how positive the clinical experiences may be, the prospect of a boiling radiator in the middle of nowhere or of sliding off the road into a snowbank in the middle of the night may severely detract from the student's appreciation of the preceptorship's health care environment. Thus, the student should be warned about potential transportation problems and advised on how to cope appropriately when they arise. Just reminding the student that gas stations are not a common item in certain rural communities, or that one must carry the exact amount of change in order to board a bus in most urban centers, may save the student a lot of time and trouble.

## COMMUNITY AND PRIMARY NURSING SCHOOL SUPPORT

After all of the above precautions have been taken by the nursing service administrator to ensure a successful student-preceptor placement, two other aspects should be considered: One is the response of the community to the student placement. Usually there will be few difficulties with the community. Racial prejudices are always a potential problem, but these can be minimized, if not extinguished, when there is active support for the student by the nursing service administrator in the health care agency's community. Such problems, which may be found more frequently in smaller communities that do not integrate different life styles or ethnic groups easily, should be dealt with individually, as they arise.

A final concern is to facilitate the support of the "mother" campus for the student and the clinical agency that accepts the student. Sometimes, the faculty of the student's primary nursing education program is apprehensive about letting go the reins on their protégé. Usually, the written documentation and evaluation of the preceptor assignment is not as clear and precise as the nursing instructors would like. The faculty may question the wisdom of allowing their student to undertake such a new clinical experiment so far away from familiar academic settings and direct academic influence, control, and evaluation. It is not uncommon for the nursing service administrator to receive a long distance telephone call from a concerned faculty member who is wondering how the student is doing. Often the faculty member merely wants to know what the student is doing clinically and how the student's goals and objectives are being met and evaluated. In such situations, it is necessary for the nursing service administrator to know exactly what the student is doing so that detailed information can be conveyed. It is not acceptable for the nursing service administrator to transfer the call of the faculty member to the student's preceptor or unit coordinator for a reply. The nursing service administrator must be prepared to answer such queries from concerned faculty members who want to make sure that their students are meeting their goals and objectives and not wasting time.

The nursing administrator's supportive and instrumental role is thus crucial in facilitating a positive student-preceptor clinical experience. The ability of the nursing service administrator to enlist the support of various support systems for the nursing student is also critical. The most important of these support systems are the nursing, medical, and ancillary hospital staffs, the chief executive officer, the governing board of directors, and various relevant community and governmental agencies. Without such support and cooperation, the nursing service administrator would have a difficult time providing a successful clinical educational experience in the student-preceptor training model.

# Chapter 20

# Administrative Support for the Preceptorship in the Clinical Setting

*Frank T. Farnkopf*

The nursing service administrator must establish a supportive administrative environment for the clinical preceptorship program. Often, nursing service administrators may underestimate the amount of control they have over the delivery of nursing care in the agency. As the title of the position implies, the nursing service administrator is the motivating force in determining the goals and direction of nursing service in the health care agency. As with all other projects in the nursing service, a positive outlook and approach by the administrator toward the preceptorship are important for its success. It is the responsibility of the administrator to facilitate this positive attitude to unite the nursing unit in creating an atmosphere that will ensure a successful preceptorship. For this reason, it is important for the administrator to establish an administrative role model that is supportive of both the student and the preceptor throughout all phases of the preceptorship.

## BASIC GROUP DYNAMICS

To avoid dissatisfaction by any of the parties involved in the preceptorship, it is necessary for the nursing service administrator to be aware of the subtle group dynamics that may occur on the nursing unit during the preceptorship. Some of the group dynamics' effects are positive. When supported appropriately by the administration, these effects can aid in providing a positive learning experience for the student and the staff involved. The effects of other group dynamics are not so positive and, unless properly acknowledged and constructively modified, may detract from the experience of the student, the preceptor, the involved staff, and the clients. These effects may involve staff rivalries, staff insecurities, personality conflicts, and student behavioral problems. In such a situation, a concerted

165

and positive effort by the nursing service administrator is required to turn counterproductive behaviors into productive interactions.

The student will be acutely aware of the fact that the student is the newest member of the health care team. Both the student and the staff will experience some anxiety and insecurity during the initial period of adjustment. The staff will be concerned that the technical and decision-making skills of the student may not meet the established standards of the nursing unit. For the student, the insecurities will stem from concerns about acceptable performance and the need to adjust to new policies, procedures, and logistics. The student will feel the burden of proving competence in an unfamiliar work environment. Until the student and staff get past this initial period of insecurity, the learning experience may be minimal for all concerned. Thus, it is important to get the student and staff past this nonproductive period rapidly. Most students will have only a limited period of time in the nursing unit. In this period, many goals and objectives must be accomplished. Thus, time is of the essence.

## STAFF SUPPORT

If the nursing staff is tuned to the dynamics of this initial period, they will probably be supportive of the new student. This will help get the student through the troublesome introductory phase and on to the more productive learning experiences and situations. In this case, little additional aid may be required of the nursing service administrator; the staff will do it all. If the administrator does not have a supportive staff, however, the administrator will personally have to help the student and the staff through the initial period. The administrator's friendliness and graciousness toward the student will set a positive role model for the staff to follow and at the same time make the student feel at ease.

Beyond the initial introduction to and support from the staff, the student should be given detailed explanations of all important or unusual unit policies and routines. With this basic information, the student will not only feel less "new" but will act more comfortably. The staff are likely to respond in kind, and anxiety levels of all parties involved will rapidly drop to normal levels.

Most staff members are likely to be considerate of the new student and will modify the environment accordingly until the student feels comfortable. There may be other staff members, however, who, for various reasons, ignore the discomfort experienced by the new student. In this situation, it is the responsibility of the nursing service administrator to help raise the awareness of those staff members who are not sensitive to the dynamics involved. The administrator can facilitate this staff consciousness raising by presenting a positive role model of acceptance, cordiality, and hospitality to the student.

Even with repeated exposure to the new student, some nursing staff members may remain insensitive to the student's anxieties. Unintentionally, they may overlook some of the things they can do to make the student feel comfortable in the new environment. Thus, it is important that the nursing service administrator continually monitor staff interactions with the new student. To repeat, a positive and hospitable attitude by the nursing service administrator will provide a role model for the nursing staff to follow.

## THE QUESTIONING STUDENT

Students often come from very large medical training centers where they were encouraged to question everything. Nursing staff members who have not been exposed to such questioning behavior often interpret and respond to it negatively. Frequently such student behavior raises staff insecurities that can result in increased staff frustration and, sometimes, in staff hostility toward the student. This could become an acute problem unless properly checked and controlled by the nursing service administrator. The administrator must help the threatened staff understand the purpose of the student's critical behavior. The staff must learn to respond to it in a positive, nonthreatened manner. They should learn to appreciate it and even encourage such questioning, since it often can give the staff greater insight into their own behavior and professionalism. It should be remembered that the student's questioning behavior is intended to broaden the student's knowledge base in competitive academic and clinical settings. Staff members who do not realize this and are affronted or intimidated by such behavior must be taught to channel their insecurities into more productive directions. A supportive administrative leadership role can be very instrumental in minimizing (if not eliminating) such counterproductive staff responses.

Infrequently, a staff member will respond to new students and staff preceptor assignments with passive or active hostile behavior, for whatever reason. For the student, such behavior can seriously damage the student-preceptor experience. In this situation, it is important for the administrator to intervene promptly with appropriate individual and group counseling to determine the cause of the inappropriate behavior. Corrective measures must be instituted promptly to prevent further harassment of the student, the preceptor, or other staff members. Unless that is done, the student will feel intimidated and come away from the preceptorship with decidedly negative views of the experience, the nursing unit, and the health care agency.

## INTERSTAFF CONFLICTS

At times, the student may be exposed to interstaff personality conflicts involving verbal attacks, gossip, rumors, innuendoes, and so on. Indeed, the potential for such behavior among members of closely-knit nursing units is always present. Here again, it is the responsibility of the nursing service administrator to identify the circumstances of the conflict and to correct the situation promptly to avoid damage to the student's learning experience.

Nursing unit settings are inherently small places. In such situations, personality conflicts are not surprising. The nursing service administrator is usually aware of these personality conflicts and thus can usefully intervene. Particularly in the case of student-preceptor assignments, it is the responsibility of the administrator to intervene in such conflicts appropriately with counseling or disciplinary action. Follow-up actions by the administrator may also include modification of the preceptor environment to spare the student who is unwittingly caught between conflicting staff or is forced to interface with unreasonable or hostile staff personalities.

If all goes well, the nursing administrator will have a staff that is completely supportive of the student's goals and objectives. This in fact is usually the rule rather than the exception. The most effective route to success is for the administrator to ensure that positive group dynamics evolve as rapidly as possible between the student and staff. The student-preceptor relationship is short-lived, and the administrator usually does not have the option of passively allowing time to heal the wounds of interstaff conflict.

## INTERACTION WITH CLIENTS

Once the nursing service administrator has ensured that the student will be exposed to optimal learning experiences and positive interactions with fellow staff, another facet of positive administrative role modeling comes into play. This involves the attitude with which medical staff, ancillary staff, and hospital administrative staff view the student interaction with clients at the health care agency. All too frequently, student participation in a clinical setting is viewed critically and negatively by powerful entities in the health care agency (for example, medical staff, board of directors, hospital administrators, ancillary department heads, and so on). Verbal reassurance from the nursing service administrator is often not enough to change these attitudes overnight. Yet, with increasing time and exposure to the student, there is often increasing trust in the student's participation by various staff entities who may have felt initially threatened. Demonstrated student competence and adequate preceptor supervision can result in a more accepting attitude toward the student in the clinical setting.

The introduction of the student to the staff of a clinical agency is particularly anxiety producing among staff members who are concerned with the legal ramifications of student error in the clinical setting. A positive supportive attitude by the nursing service administrator can dramatically overcome these initial apprehensions.

It is important for the nursing service administrator to inform concerned staff of the many positive aspects of student participation. In their facility, the authors have observed that:

- Students document the patient care they perform in a more thorough and concise manner.
- As a rule, students approach clients in a more careful and objective manner.
- Students often have a more current and thus more effective professional approach.
- Students are always under the supervision of a trusted staff member.
- Students are in a clinical setting to learn and not just put in eight hours for pay.
- Students often have their own professional licensure (for example, as a registered nurse) and thus are aware of and accountable for their actions under their own particular nursing practice act.

These findings provide substantial justification for student participation in the clinical setting. The apprehension of other professional services and administrative entities often stems from fear of the unknown and the unproven. Over time, the students will become an accepted and trusted addition to the clinical setting. Until this accepting climate evolves, however, a positive and supportive attitude by the nursing service administrator is essential.

## STAFF MISUSE OF THE STUDENT

A situation that the nursing service administrator must avoid is that in which the distinction between the unpaid student role and the unpaid staff role becomes blurred. Particularly in this day of chronic health care man-power shortages, staff may unwittingly begin to utilize the student as a staff member. Frequently students will allow this to happen at the expense of their goals and objectives for clinical placement and participation.

It is also important that the regular health care staff avoid viewing the trusted student as a volunteer. The time that the student spends in the health care agency is limited. There is thus an emphasis on the successful accomplishment of the student's goals and objectives as quickly as possible. Out of appreciation, the student may be agreeable to "helping out" the staff, which may be chronically short in numbers and overworked. Unfor-tunately, this is usually done at the expense of the student's academic needs.

It is important that the nursing service administrator be attuned to these possible sidetrackings and intervene accordingly. Usually, reminding the staff of the student's unpaid status and academic requirements will solve the problem relatively painlessly, without the student being aware of the administrator's unsolicited intervention.

## COMMUNITY RELATIONS

Strong administrative support of the preceptorship model is also required of the nursing service director in community and governmental circles. While strong in-house administrative support of the student and preceptor is important to the success of the student and preceptor relationship, the cultivation of positive public relations with community and governmental organizations is important to justify ongoing federally (or politically) funded preceptor programs. This may involve justification of ongoing pilot projects with eventual expansion into larger programs. The justification may be required at grass-roots community levels as well as at more general state-wide and national governmental levels.

Such demonstrated administrative support by the nursing service direc-tor, whether it be directed at the local or federal levels, is crucial in in-creasing awareness of the valuable academic experience that nursing stu-dents gain through a preceptor model. The relevant public relations produced by the nursing service administrator can take the form of news media interviews, guest speaking assignments, video or written documentation and publication, or informal collaboration with similar agencies that are attempting to establish preceptor clinical arrangements for students.

Other types of support may be in the form of increased involvement with community and governmental agencies, written statements of support specifically addressed to key legislators, and academic financial support of preceptor programs. The supportive nursing service administrator can also address small business and industry and other institutions of higher education to increase their awareness of the goals and objectives of preceptorship programs. Any area of the community or state that is involved with the hospital is an appropriate target for soliciting support. Often the administrator is in a key political position to address the various levels of community, government, and academia as to the importance of promoting student preceptor assignments and relationships. In these ways, administrators can utilize their positions to further education from the classroom to the clinical setting through the student-preceptor model.

## LEARNING OBJECTIVES

Finally and most importantly, a supportive administrative role model can stimulate the student toward creative individual expression as exposure to the clinical nursing unit increases. It is important that the student feel comfortable with personal expression in meeting personal academic and social goals and objectives. Here the nursing administrator should make clear to the student, the preceptor, and other involved parties that the nursing administrative framework encourages individual student behavior based upon goals and objectives that meet the academic needs of the student.

The administrator should also encourage the student to feel flexible in modifying established goals and objectives. Indeed, new experiences and opportunities may require modification of the original goals and objectives throughout the clinical preceptorship. The goals and objectives will become more appropriate as continued clinical exposure provides more input.

All participants in the student-preceptor experience must understand and encourage the model's dynamic and changing modalities. As we have seen, the dynamic interplay of individuals includes not only the student and the preceptor but also the staff that interfaces with the student and the preceptor at all levels of the patient care delivery system. It also of course involves the nursing service administrator. Without this interplay of administrative support, a successful preceptorship of student clinical learning experiences is not possible.

# Part V

# Refining the Preceptorship Program—A Shared Responsibility

# Chapter 21

# Evaluation in Preceptorship Programs

*Diane Rowe*

Evaluation is an ongoing process that is based upon an established set of criteria and standards of performance that has been cooperatively developed to measure the learner's behavior. Primarily, the intent of evaluation is to provide descriptive data that will allow an explanation of current status and promote necessary alterations. Estimations and appraisals are components of evaluation; hence it is a process of making value judgments about knowledge, skills, and attitudes to form a realistic basis for effective change.

The purpose of this chapter is not to de-emphasize the traditional evaluative practices recognized by educators as important components of any nursing curriculum. Rather, the purpose is to introduce and examine the concept of preceptorship evaluation as an enhancement of the traditional method. Preceptors add a new dimension to this procedure by incorporating a third person into the customary two-person evaluative interaction.

## THE EVALUATION PROCESS

### Evaluation As a Conceptual Process

One of the major issues confronting nursing education today is how to increase the effectiveness of the clinical experience provided for students. Various means have been explored to seek better quality learning situations for the student. The nursing profession has had to expand and specialize to cope with current explosions of theories and concepts of nursing practice. These fast-paced changes have put a burden on the role of nurse educators who may have graduate degrees in a nursing field such as medical-surgical. These educators are recognizing that it is impossible for them to maintain skills in areas such as intensive care, coronary care, dialysis, and emergency nursing while at the same time fulfilling faculty obligations. To deal with this problem, many nurse educators are choosing to utilize nurses who have expertise in other specialty areas. Indeed, the educator's role can be enhanced by utilizing other members of the profession who are currently practicing in a variety of specialized fields. The term *preceptor* has been applied to such a person, someone who has been carefully selected by the nurse educator to serve as an adjunct to the faculty role.

The concept of a preceptorship is, however, not readily accepted by all nurse educators. An explanation of the reluctance to accept preceptorships is related to apprenticeship practices that were common in nursing education prior to World War II. At that time, students were placed in clinical settings where their experiences were selected and supervised by a staff nurse or by one of their peers. In many instances, the clinical supervisors were other members of their own class who had recently completed the service, or they were staff nurses with clinical expertise whose job it was to see that the students completed assignments in time to attend class. In either case, nurse educators began to realize that the focus of the assignment was not on meeting student learning objectives but rather in giving service to the institution.

The difference today is that educators in nursing no longer accept apprenticeship practices. When a student is placed in an institution under the supervision of a preceptor, the entire focus is on the student's learning. The preceptorship experience is educationally based, and the responsible nurse educator ensures that the preceptor's purpose is to work in concert with both educator and student toward the educational goal.

To ensure that education is the major goal, a conceptual framework is designed by the nursing educator to guide and direct the preceptor in the evaluator's role to meet the course objectives. Seminars and individual meetings are integral parts of the preparation and orientation of the preceptor with regard to the educator's expectations, the student's role, and the importance of the preceptor's input through ongoing evaluation. Eventually, the preceptor's last written evaluation is incorporated into the educator's final evaluation.

To assist the preceptor in fulfilling the role of evaluator, the educator has the responsibility, through frequent contacts, to guide the preceptor in carrying out the preceptorship assignment. Direct contact is maintained through site visits to the agency, during which the educator is present with the preceptor and/or the student. It can be assumed that most practicing nurse/clinician preceptors have not had advanced preparation in the theories and principles of evaluation. Therefore, the preceptor will need direction and supervision in gathering data that can be used to formulate a complete appraisal.

The site visits have a dual purpose: First, they provide a learning experience for the preceptors as they expand their knowledge base from that of a practicing nurse to that of an evaluating nurse. Second, they provide a support system to facilitate the evaluation process. Additionally, when the preceptor, student, and educator meet together as established by the course guidelines, the preceptor becomes a vital element in the educational process. Upon assuming a role in the process, the preceptor's evaluation becomes a valid input that can be used by the nursing educator in the formulation of a grade.

## Evaluation As an Integral Process

The necessity for evaluation is inherent in any educational program or course of study. It is an integral process that provides feedback relative either to maintaining the status quo or to cultivating change. When a preceptor becomes involved in a course as an evaluator, the end result contributes to a broader based appraisal. This expanded concept is a dynamically directed transaction that has three main constituents: evaluation of self, evaluation of the preceptor by the student, and evaluation of the student by the preceptor.

The first of four criteria for evaluating oneself is that related to role modeling. Role modeling behaviors are professionalism, self-responsibility, accountability, clinical expertise, and peer acceptance.

The second criterion deals with evaluating oneself as a resource person. This role is probably the most familiar one, and also probably the most overused. One's expert knowledge and skill should be shared with the student. However, other resources—such as the library, clinical findings, and independent functions—should not be overlooked. Clarity of explanation and return demonstrations are also important learning tools.

The third criterion is that of a designer of instruction. This role involves a formal approach to the structure of the teaching-learning interaction between the preceptor and the student. Expectations, objectives, educational experiences, plans for evaluation, and orientation to the agency setting are all components of instruction.

The fourth and last criterion of self-evaluation is that of a supervisor. This role is one of facilitation, the primary goal being to enhance the student's professional autonomy. Clinical supervision demands a passive role for the preceptor and an active role for the student, as the dependent-independent-interdependent relationship develops.

The second constituent is the student's evaluation of the preceptor's performance. This is based on the same criteria that are used in self-evaluation. The student is more likely to evaluate positively those traits in the preceptor that relate to role modeling when there is mutual support and concern for learning needs. Likewise, the student will recognize the shared experience and instructional methods employed by the preceptor as positive factors when evaluating those areas. The preceptor's supervisory skills are generally seen by the student as essential to the student's learning needs and will therefore be ranked in the light of the relationship between the authority exercised and the knowledge gained. Use of the same criteria by both preceptor and student results in a more meaningful appraisal for review by the nursing educator.

The third constituent, that of the preceptor's evaluation of the student, is the most important in the evaluative process. The criteria that must be met to complete this evaluation are student-formulated learning objectives as approved by both instructor and preceptor, established course objectives, and terminal objectives as identified by the curriculum. In order to assist in achieving the student's learning objectives and to maximize the student's learning activities, the preceptor must be comfortable with the student's objectives. The preceptor should be realistic about the objectives and share thoughts with the student and the educator as to the availability of learning activities in the agency. The student-prepared learning objectives must also be approved by the nurse educator, in order to promote the interfacing of established course objectives and the terminal objectives of the curriculum. Once the student's objectives are finalized, they are used as a guide for the student's clinical experience. It is the responsibility of the educator to maintain both student and preceptor contacts through site visits to ensure that the three criteria for the preceptor's evaluation of the student are met.

### Evaluation As an Indirect Process

Preceptorships add a new dimension to the evaluative process. The flexibility of student placements, a variety of student prepared learning objectives, and the involvement of preceptors serve to amplify the traditional educator-student evaluation process. As experiences are individualized for the student and directed by the preceptor, the educator is placed in the difficult position of maintaining control over the evaluation process. However, the negative effects of relaxed control by the educator are minimized by the positive aspects of expanded learning opportunities for the student. By utilizing preceptors, students are allowed greater freedom to select learning experiences that can motivate them to perform and achieve. The preceptors, for their part, share their expertise in the teacher role with the students. This enhances the preceptor's role modeling behaviors, since they are able to see a student grow and mature in knowledge and skill under their direction.

The student-teacher ratio is maximized in a preceptor course when one educator coordinates as many as 20 to 24 students with an equal number of preceptors. This large student load dictates a more passive, indirect role for the educator, not only in terms of supervision but in relation to evaluation as well. As the educator assumes a more indirect role in evaluation, the student role in the process is maximized, as the students accept direct responsibility for learning outcomes.

Contemporary observations in education provide evidence that student input is essential to decrease the subjective aspect of evaluation. Subjectivity is further decreased when the third person, the preceptor, is involved. The preceptor tends to be free of bias, since the issuance of a grade is not within the scope of the preceptor's established responsibilities. Evaluation thus becomes more objective, since three persons are making value judgments about knowledge, skills, and attitudes.

Although the educator assumes a less direct role in the evaluative function, statistics indicate that it is very beneficial to have both student input and an unbiased appraisal by the preceptor of the student's performance. These data, coupled with educator input, create an effective means for reducing subjectivity and increasing objectivity in the evaluative process.

## CONTRACT GRADING, A TOOL IN THE EVALUATION PROCESS

We have seen that the preceptorship experience deviates from the traditional experience in which the nurse educator directly supervises the student's learning. In a preceptorship, the educator is absent except during site visits to the agency. This can create a problem when a grade must be determined that covers the student's learning experience. One solution is to use contract grading. This new and innovative approach to the age-old problem of grade assignment has been found to be an effective means of involving students and teachers in a mutual decision-making role.

A grade contract is a flexible system that allows freedom to students in grade selection. Contracts can be one, or a combination, of three types: open, semiopen, and closed. An open contract allows a student to select a grade based on a written set of criteria; the designated grade is thus formulated by the student. The educator reviews the contract with the student to determine approval or disapproval, and the discussion then ends in mutual agreement. It is difficult to control an open contract due to a lack of educator-defined criteria for grading. However, this method of grading has the largest student input.

The semiopen contract differs from the open contract in that there is a minimal set of established criteria. The student has options with which to determine how the criteria will be met, and guidelines are established for the various options. The student then fulfills the selected assignment in order to earn the selected grade. Closed contracts allow the student to choose a grade according to a predetermined set of criteria, but with no option to add to those criteria.

An advantage of the contract grading process is that the student is given freedom to change the grade. At any time, if it becomes impossible or undesirable to meet the contracted grade level, the student has the option to contract for a lower grade. Similarly, within a given time frame, the student has the option to raise the grade level if it is possible and desirable to complete additional assignments according to established guidelines of the contract.

## A TYPICAL EVALUATION PROCESS

Preceptorship courses are rapidly becoming a new trend in nursing education. Such courses enhance the learning experiences of the students and enable nursing curricula to offer a wider variety of clinical placements to the students.

An example of a preceptorship course is that of the Senior Clinical Focus Course (SCFC) at California State University, Fresno, which began in the spring of 1980. This course has a two-unit theory component (referred to as senior focus) that is offered concurrently with a three-unit clinical component. The SCFC, placed in the curriculum at the second semester senior level, requires 135 clinical contact hours. The students have completed public health nursing; therefore, they have had community-based as well as acute care experiences.

SCFC faculty meet with the community health nursing students at midterm to introduce the concepts of the course and some of the rural and urban options available to them for clinical placement in the SCFC. Virtually any area of nursing within the service area of the campus is a possible option for the students. If the agency is willing to provide a qualified preceptor and can offer the student the best learning situation, the option will be considered.

At this point, an application is presented, and returns are requested within two weeks. Hopefully, the two-week period will allow the students time to decide on a focus area and an agency of interest. The application gives the SCFC faculty a general idea about the student's background and past experiences, as well as first and second choices of desired focus areas and agencies for the upcoming semester. The applications are then divided among the SCFC faculty, who make the agency contacts and assist in the preceptor selection process.

The ratio of students to faculty is approximately 21:1. Placements within agencies and the selection of preceptors are generally completed by the end of the semester prior to the semester in which the student is to begin. This advanced preparation alerts the agency to requested areas and the preceptors required. It also allows the students to make contact with the agency and preceptor in order to prepare the required learning objectives prior to school vacations. The students have the opportunity to formulate a set of realistic learning objectives and related learning activities with preceptor input. The students can then prepare a tentative schedule of hours that is convenient for both student and preceptor.

Preceptor seminars are offered two or three times a year to orient new and interested preceptors to the SCFC. The seminars also provide related topics of interest to the returning preceptors, while offering them continuing education credits as well. The preceptors are given the same packets of course materials that the students receive. Ideally, all of the preceptors are oriented and ready to begin their role when the new semester begins.

The students are required to finalize their learning objectives and turn in a schedule of the days and hours they will be working at the beginning of the SCFC. A sample format of learning objectives is given to the students for use in preparing and finalizing their own objectives. The learning objectives should reflect realistic personal and professional goals and objectives and related activities appropriate to the student placement facility. Students have almost unlimited flexibility in selecting a clinical schedule. Some choose to continue with night hours or weekend shifts, while others are committed to specific hours within their preceptor's schedule or their agency's working hours.

The SCFC objectives are broad, general, holistic nursing concepts that are designed to be appropriate to any area of nursing selected by the students and to interface with the terminal objectives of the curriculum. The course objectives require (1) a set of student-prepared learning objectives to guide the student in the clinical learning experience, (2) a log book or written communication, and (3) a grade contract. Copies of the learning objectives are distributed to SCFC faculty, the preceptor, and the preceptor's immediate supervisor. Hopefully, this helps to initiate learning guidance for the student in the agency. Once the SCFC faculty receives copies of the objectives and schedules, a master schedule is formulated to coordinate the student load for site visits with the availability of students and preceptors. At the same time, preparations are made for the following semester's students.

Students maintain a written communication system by means of a log into which entries are made after each clinical experience. The log has three components of learning: cognitive, affective, and psychomotor. Through use of the log, the faculty follow the experiences and learning processes of each student and can provide ongoing written feedback. The log is made available during site visits and upon request for faculty review. Another purpose of the log is to keep an accurate record of the hours completed toward the required 135 hours.

Grade contracts are used in a semiopen mode with options for a grade of A, B, or C. The criteria established for a minimum of C are student-prepared learning objectives, maintenance of a log, satisfactory clinical performance, and a grade contract. A B grade requires the criteria for a C grade (excellence in clinical performance) and in addition a six-hour, continuing education course related to the student's focus area. A critique of the continuing education course is also required. Requisites for an A grade include the C and B grade criteria and, in addition, a project or report on a topic of interest related to the student's focus area. Guidelines for clinical performance, projects, and papers are outlined, and the project topic requires approval by the SCFC faculty. A copy of the SCFC grade contract is presented as Exhibit 21–1.

Evaluations of the clinical component are completed by both student and preceptor and reviewed by the SCFC faculty in consideration of the grade contract prior to issuing the final grade. The students evaluate their own performance according to the course objectives. The course objectives are evaluated on a holistic scale that includes a range from self to inter-planetary. This tool allows the student (with input from the preceptor and faculty) to evaluate the levels at which each course objective was met. Every student should minimally have attained the level of "self" for each objective. For most of the objectives, the majority of students evaluate themselves through the "community" areas of the evaluation. This eval-uation tool can be loosely interpreted; the cumulative results vary widely among the students. A copy of the SCFC format for evaluating course objectives is presented as Exhibit 21–2.

Evaluative summaries are written by each student at the completion of the course, following established summary guidelines as shown in Exhibit 21–3. A copy of this summary is sent to the agency as feedback on the student's experience.

The students are also evaluated by the preceptor, using the format shown in Exhibit 21–4. Better response has been noted when a preestablished form is available.

Concurrently, the students evaluate the preceptors using four criteria: role model, resource person, designer of instruction, and supervisor. The

**Exhibit 21-1** SCFC Grade Contract

CALIFORNIA STATE UNIVERSITY, FRESNO
Department of Nursing

NURSING 128BL

**GRADE CONTRACT**

*Grade*

C    1. Write learning objectives with specific activities and reading assignments.
2. Perform satisfactorily in the clinical setting as defined in the course objectives and follow guidelines pertaining to student responsibilities in focus experience.
3. Keep a daily log including hours, activities and interpretation of cognitive, affective and motor-skill learnings.

B    1. Meet criteria for C grade.
2. Attend a workshop or inservice class related to focus area, (minimum of 6 hours). A typed, well-written summary and critique is required (3-4 pages)
3. Exhibit excellence in the clinical area.

A    1. Meet criteria for B grade.
2. Project, paper, etc., determined by student with instructor approval.

All course work is due to the instructor no later than _____ .
Weaknesses in any area may result in lowering of grade.

I, _____ , hereby agree to meet the grading criteria as stated in the course outline for Nursing 128BL and written by _____ ,
my instructor. I further agree to contract for a grade of _____ . I understand that I may recontract at any time for a lower grade, but must have ample time to complete the requirements to recontract for a higher grade. Attached or on the back of this sheet I have enumerated what I will do to earn the selected grade.

_____    _____
Student                            Date

_____    _____
Instructor                         Date

*Source:* Senior Clinical Focus Faculty. Fresno, Calif.: California State University, Department of Nursing.

preceptors receive this evaluation after it is reviewed by the faculty. Student input from these preceptor evaluations is retained for future preceptor selection. A copy of the SCFC form for student evaluation of preceptors is presented as Exhibit 21-5.

Original copies of the course objective evaluation, the student's summary of the experience, and the preceptor's evaluation of the student are placed

**Exhibit 21–2** SCFC Format for Evaluating Course Objectives

CALIFORNIA STATE UNIVERSITY, FRESNO
Department of Nursing

NURSING 128BL - EVALUATION OF COURSE OBJECTIVES

*Objectives:*

Broad professional and personal development objectives provide a standard for student performance. These objectives are met within a variety of relationships, i.e. with oneself, peers, clients, their families, the clinical setting and its staff, and many levels of community. These community levels include local, state, national, international and interplanetary.

Upon completion of N128BL the student will have demonstrated on at least one relationship level each of the following objectives:

| | Self | Peers | Clients | Families | Staff/Agency | Local | County | State | Nation | International | Interplanetary |
|---|---|---|---|---|---|---|---|---|---|---|---|
| | | | | | | COMMUNITY | | | | | |
| I. A humanistic approach to nursing practice with individuals and groups. | | | | | | | | | | | |
| 1. Demonstrates a regular pattern of respect for individual rights and differences. | | | | | | | | | | | |
| 2. Demonstrates a regular pattern of behavior showing sensitivity to needs of individuals of diverse cultural backgrounds. | | | | | | | | | | | |
| 3. Attempts to assist peers, coworkers and clients to achieve their potential for wellness and growth. | | | | | | | | | | | |
| 4. Attempts to serve as an advocate for individuals and groups. | | | | | | | | | | | |
| II. Growth and independence of thought and action as a responsible professional practitioner. | | | | | | | | | | | |
| 1. Demonstrates awareness of own values and how they may affect practice with culturally different clients and coworkers. | | | | | | | | | | | |
| 2. Is reliable in meeting obligations to clients, staff, and faculty. | | | | | | | | | | | |
| 3. Demonstrates awareness of own limitations in knowledge and skills by seeking guidance from appropriate persons. | | | | | | | | | | | |
| 4. Utilizes available opportunities and resources to meet learning objectives. | | | | | | | | | | | |
| 5. Accepts responsibility for own actions and educational experiences. | | | | | | | | | | | |

**Exhibit 21–2** continued

|  | Self | Peers | Clients | Families | Staff/Agency | Local | County | State | Nation | International | Interplanetary |
|---|---|---|---|---|---|---|---|---|---|---|---|
|  |  |  |  |  |  | COMMUNITY | | | | | |

III. Knowledge of present and emerging professional nursing roles and responsibilities in changing health.
1. Recognizes potential for developing new professional nursing roles.
2. Recognizes effects of change on traditional nursing roles and relationships.
3. Consults practitioners in other disciplines about problems in the delivery of health care.

IV. A systematic approach to problem solving and decision making in identifying and meeting needs of oneself, other individuals and groups in a health care delivery system.
1. Utilizes a systematic approach in the analysis of problems which arise in the clinical setting and related areas.
2. Analyzes the consequences of alternative solutions to problems encountered in the clinical setting and related areas.
3. Proposes appropriate referrals for clinical problems outside the scope of nursing responsibilities.

V. Knowledge of biological, psychological, and social influences on health as a basis for understanding changes in health care and health care delivery systems.
1. Demonstrates awareness of social, economic and political changes that affect the health care problems within the various levels of community.
2. Analyzes the multicultural aspects of health care problems within the community.

VI. Application of principles of communication, group dynamics, change and learning theories to goal-oriented relationships with individuals and groups.

## Exhibit 21–2 continued

|  | Self | Peers | Clients | Families | Staff/Agency | Local | County | State | Nation | International | Interplanetary |
|---|---|---|---|---|---|---|---|---|---|---|---|
|  |  |  |  |  |  | COMMUNITY | | | | | |

1. Utilizes principles from group dynamics when working at the placement facility and related areas.
2. Uses effective communication skills when interacting with persons in various relationships.
3. Utilizes appropriate channels of communication.
4. Demonstrates awareness of own behavior in group interactions and in teaching-learning situations.

VII. Understanding of leadership in health care systems and services and in the achievement of individual, group, agency, and societal goals.
1. Demonstrates understanding of the agency's relationship to the broader society and its government, its organizational structure, goals, policies, and sources of power and conflict.
2. Identifies approaches used by the health care organizations to deal with conflict.
3. Participates in a variety of agency activities—as well as related areas of interest.
4. Understands the working roles of agency personnel and of those in the health care delivery systems and its community.
5. Functions within the agency rules and regulations.
6. Appearance and behavior are appropriate to the clinical setting and community.

VIII. Understanding of the role of theory and research in the study and solution of problems in nursing practice.
1. Identifies problems within the organization suitable for nursing research.

*Source:* Holy Names College, Department of Nursing. Oakland, Calif.

**Exhibit 21–3** SCFC Summary Guidelines

CALIFORNIA STATE UNIVERSITY, FRESNO
Department of Nursing

N 128BL - Senior Clinical Focus in Nursing

**SUMMARY OF N 128BL EXPERIENCE**

At the seminars, you have all had a chance to share with us your experiences in your placement site; experiences that involved your preceptor, some continuity of care impressions, and the community as a whole.

Thinking about the total experience, re-state in summary your final impressions now that it is over. Include your reactions to the following questions in your response:

1. Why was it, or was it not a valuable experience to have at *this time* in your educational program? In what ways do you predict this preceptorship experience will influence your future plans for job selection? Continued academic growth?
2. Compare your understanding of how health care is provided in a rural area before participation in N 128BL and after participation (if applicable).
3. Do you recommend this as a learning experience for another student? What are your reasons?
4. Preceptor relationship: What were the most helpful factors of your relationship with your preceptor? What were the least helpful factors of your relationship with your preceptor?
5. Were your community experiences useful? Did you become better acquainted with the community? What other experiences would you have liked?
6. Instructor/student: What were the most helpful/least helpful factors of your relationship with CSUF instructor? Roles, site visits, seminars, and communication? What recommendations do you have for improving the instructor/student relationship?
7. What do you feel was unique about this clinical placement experience?

*Source:* Rural Clinical Nurse Placement Center. Chico, Calif.: California State University.

in the student's file at the completion of the course. During the final evaluation, the faculty and student review these evaluations, and each is signed and dated by both parties. In addition, a letter of thanks is sent to each preceptor by the SCFC faculty, along with the student's evaluation summary, as a small reward for their great service to the students and the learning institution.

## CONCLUSION

Evaluation is a component part of a larger process, for example, the nursing process. However, it is also a process within itself. The evaluation process as used in a preceptorship course can be viewed in a conceptual framework as an ongoing process based upon an established set of criteria

**Exhibit 21–4** SCFC Form for Preceptor Evaluation of Student

California State University Fresno Dept. of Nursing
N128BL Senior Clinical Focus
Preceptor's Evaluation of Student

Student's Name _____ Placement Dates: _____

1. What are your observations about:
   a. the student's performance

   b. preceptor/agency satisfactions with the senior focus program

2. What were the most positive features of the experience:

3. What were the least positive features of the experience:

4. What are your recommendations to improve the student's placement experience:

5. If you had a job opening for which this person were qualified, would you employ this student after he/she graduated: Yes_____ No_____ Why:

6. Additional comments:

Name of person writing evaluation: _____ Agency:_____
                                                              Date:_____

*Source:* Rural Clinical Nurse Placement Center. Chico, Calif.: California State University.

and performance standards that has been cooperatively developed to measure the learner's behavior.

An indirect evaluative role is assumed by the nurse educator, who traditionally has conducted unilateral evaluations of students. This new approach provides much less subjectivity and enhances the objectivity of the evaluation through involvement of a third person and the maximization of student input into the evaluation process. Contract grading has been found to be an effective way to deal with the problem of grade assignment in

**Exhibit 21–5** SCFC Form for Student Evaluation of Preceptor

I. *The Preceptor as a Role Model:*
   1. How many times did your preceptor meet with you, and did she/he allow you an exchange of feedback?

   2. Did you feel there was open communication and trust between you and your preceptor?

   3. Did your preceptor offer you support? How?

II. *The Preceptor as a Resource Person:*
   1. Discuss your preceptor with respect to the following areas:
      a. Willingness to share her/his expertise

      b. Demonstration of procedures, etc., when appropriate

      c. Assistance in finding other resources when appropriate

      d. Clarity of demonstrations and explanations. Did you give feedback to your preceptor?

III. *The Preceptor as a Designer of Instruction:*
   1. Discuss your preceptor with respect to the following aspects of your placement:
      a. Orientation to facility by preceptor

      b. Introduction to the staff

      c. Discussion of each other's expectations from the learning experience

   2. Did you feel accepted? Did you feel a part of the staff?

   3. Did your preceptor analyze, with you, the meaning of your objectives?

   4. Was your preceptor able to provide useful and interesting experiences to meet your objectives?

   5. Did your preceptor plan the educational experiences with you, or did you do this independently?

   6. Was there optimum use of your time?

   7. Based on the agreed-upon objectives and the plan for implementing the instruction, did both you and your preceptor participate in ongoing evaluation of your progress? Did you find this evaluation satisfactory?

   8. Did your preceptor help you become acquainted with, and understand, her/his unique rural community? How?

**Exhibit 21–5** continued

IV. *The Preceptor as a Supervisor:*
   1. Did you feel your preceptor provided appropriate supervision?
      Academic?
      Clinical?

   2. Did she/he have weekly conferences with you? Did you feel they were satisfactory?

   3. Did she/he impose her/his viewpoint on you?

   4. Did she/he encourage self-initiation, individuality, self-expression, and self-evaluation? How?

 V. During this preceptorship experience, was your preceptor able to employ the four teaching roles?

VI. Describe in what ways she/he excelled as a preceptor and how she/he could improve as a teacher:

Student _____Preceptor _____Placement Date _____

*Source:* Simon, M.P.A. *A role guide and resource book for clinical preceptors.* Washington, D.C.: U.S. Government Printing Office, 1976; and Rural Clinical Nurse Placement Center. Chico, Calif.: California State University.

this dependent-independent-interdependent student role. Based on these concepts, the type of preceptorship course exemplified by the SCFC has grown in popularity with students and community agencies and has become an integral part of the nursing curriculum.

# Chapter 22

# Preceptor Seminars and Their Use in the Nursing Education Program

*Phyllis Schubert*

Preceptor seminars are planned educational experiences for nurses and physicians who have accepted the responsibility of serving as role models, supervisors, resource persons, and designers of instruction for nursing students in health care agency settings. Faculty members involved with the preceptors plan and conduct the seminars. Preceptors, students, faculty members, and other selected persons from the university or community are involved in various aspects of the seminars. The overall goal is orientation for new preceptors and continuing education to improve the quality of the learning experiences for nursing students. The seminars are most frequently held at university sites, but they could be held in any accessible community setting.

In this chapter we shall explore (1) the purpose of preceptor seminars, (2) factors in selecting content and teaching methods, (3) the seminar's logistics, and (4) evaluation of the experience.

## THE PURPOSE OF PRECEPTOR SEMINARS

The general purpose of preceptor seminars is to meet the needs of the instructor, preceptors, and students. The primary need of the instructor may be the efficient use of resources of time, money, and energy. A group of preceptors can be oriented to the program and its expectations in a few hours, whereas on a one-to-one basis the same orientation could take many weeks and thousands of driving miles, especially in rural areas. It still is necessary, of course, for the instructor to provide orientation to new preceptors who are unable to attend the seminars.

The instructor often finds, too, that the seminars are more effective than one-to-one sessions because preceptors learn from each other. Teaching and learning are reinforced by the participants through small and large

191

group discussions. Another benefit of the seminar is the feedback the instructor or coordinator receives through the program evaluation process. This feedback is a valuable resource for program planning.

Seminars also provide the opportunity for appreciation to be expressed to the preceptors for their contributions to the students' learning and to the educational program. Creative ways of recognizing these efforts might include direct expressions of gratitude by the instructor, department chairpersons, deans, or the president of the university. Refreshments, pleasant atmosphere, certificates and awards, continuing education credit for the time spent in the seminar, lunches, and parking arrangements are among the myriad of things that can be provided to help express appreciative feelings. This aspect of the seminar deserves careful thought and planning.

The students benefit by having prepared and confident preceptors who are able to create positive learning environments for the students in a short period of time. Confident and knowledgeable preceptors help the students to experience less anxiety and to acquire a sense of security and trust. Such an atmosphere is conducive to learning and to meeting goals and objectives.

Students may also be involved in the seminar for preceptors by presenting summaries of projects, by planning group presentations with preceptors on relevant topics and issues, and by helping with the logistics of the seminar and with refreshments. The sharing of experiences and insights can be meaningful for both students and preceptors. In this way, students can experience an increased sense of identification with the nursing profession. The sense of cooperation, unity, and identity is enhanced as the students work together with representatives of nursing service and education to present their ideas to each other.

Preceptors seem to feel the seminars are helpful in several ways. First, the preceptors are given an opportunity to meet with other preceptors and to benefit from their shared experiences with students. Preceptors also enjoy partnerships with nurse educators in the task of educating students. The seminars give preceptors an opportunity to meet with faculty and university personnel, and they provide feedback and ideas for planning to improve the educational program. As contributors to the program, such persons are respected, and their ideas are carefully considered in implementation of curriculum. The accumulation of continuing education units is also valued by the preceptors. A final benefit is the nurse preceptor's exposure to continuous changes in the profession.

## FACTORS IN SELECTING CONTENT AND TEACHING METHODS

Planning for group experiences that include mutual sharing and learning demands creativity, flexibility within a framework, and sensitivity to the needs of the persons involved. The seminar must possess a dynamic quality, evidenced by an interchange of ideas.

A variety of teaching-learning modes may be utilized. Lectures, small and large group discussions, role plays, skits, demonstrations, and a variety of visual aids provide a context for an interesting learning experience. Small groups composed of preceptors and students may plan to present a topic. For example, those involved in maternal/child nursing might present an aspect of bonding or discuss a current legislative effort affecting the practice of midwifery. Those involved in rehabilitative nursing may present a proposal for support groups by which encouragement is received from peers in the work setting. Such a program requires the instructor to serve as a facilitator and resource person for the students and preceptors who determine the content and methodology of the presentation. The instructor may be asked by one of the groups to be involved in a group learning activity. Another approach may be to have student and preceptor projects and experiences presented by individuals, pairs, or groups. These presentations may be a part of the program involving students. The remaining time may be used for preceptor instruction, discussion, and interaction.

The seminar site and the length of time allotted for the seminar should be determined by the needs of the participants, the content to be presented, and the activities to be included. Timing is also a critical factor and may determine the attendance. Monday mornings, for example, seem to be especially inappropriate for nursing staff members to attend seminars, whereas Wednesday afternoons have been found to be conducive to larger attendance.

The development of a preceptor seminar is part of an evolutionary process. The content and the context change with each meeting, due to changing needs of participants, changing perceptions of those needs, and flashes of creative inspiration by some preceptors, students, or faculty. The participants' evaluations of the seminars are thoroughly reviewed for suggestions to improve the sessions and to provide meaningful content.

The faculty at California State University, Fresno Department of Nursing, have developed a four-hour seminar. Two hours involve students and include preceptor group presentations of selected topics and issues. Interested students, faculty, and members of the community are invited to attend. The third hour is used to orient the new preceptors and a seminar for the others. This hour is focused on a theoretical presentation of a nursing concept presented in the students' coursework that may need clarification and expansion for the preceptors. The two groups then meet together in the fourth hour to share thoughts and ideas in a structured exercise designed to stimulate interaction between new preceptors and those with experience in preceptoring. The afternoon is summarized by representatives of the individual groups who report considerations and observations to the whole group under the direction of the instructor or someone else selected to perform that task. Evaluation forms are completed and posttest questions are answered to satisfy continuing education requirements.

This format is just one stage in the evolutionary process. The content must be updated and readapted continuously in order to provide a challenging learning experience for preceptors who choose to continue their involvement with the program in future seminars.

## LOGISTICS OF A PRECEPTOR SEMINAR

The following eight steps are involved in setting up a continuing education program for preceptors:

1. Assess the needs of the preceptors, instructors and students for effective student learning. Data for these assessments should be collected from each of the sources and then prioritized for the seminar. Much of the assessment data will come from suggestions made in personal contacts during preceptor/student/instructor conferences and faculty group discussions and from evaluation forms from previous seminars.
2. Develop objectives to meet the identified needs.
3. Plan the program so that the objectives can be met through interesting and pleasant learning experiences. Content identified with appropriate methods is used to provide the context for learning. Aspects of the program—such as speaking, assisting, ordering equipment, preparing materials, and leading discussions—are assigned. The date and time require careful planning to accommodate the greatest number of people. The time must correspond with the efforts and objectives of the instructors and students involved.
4. Select a room with the desired learning environment. For example, stationary chairs would not facilitate a small group discussion.
5. Send invitations six to eight weeks in advance in order to facilitate attendance. The invitation should include the logistical information of what, who, when, where, and why, as well as the objectives and/or the program. A warm message of appreciation and encouragement may be included in the invitation. An RSVP form may also be included to aid in preparation for the appropriate number of persons. An example of a seminar invitation and program is shown in Exhibit 22–1.

**Exhibit 22–1** Preceptor Seminar Invitation and Program

CALIFORNIA STATE UNIVERSITY, FRESNO
Department of Nursing

March 18, 1982

*MEMORANDUM*

TO: Preceptors for Senior Clinical Focus

FROM: Senior Clinical Focus Faculty
Schubert, Rowe, Boehm and Sacksteder

SUBJECT: Preceptor/Student Seminar

WHEN: Wednesday, May 5, 1982
1:00–5:00 p.m.

WHERE: Old Cafeteria, Room 200 (upstairs)
Parking available in Lot C unrestricted.

WHAT: All preceptors—past, present, and interested—are invited and encouraged to attend.

Continuing Education Units (4) will be provided for those Registered Nurses who attend the whole session.

*OBJECTIVES:*

Upon completion of the seminar, participants will have
1. Shared in the presentation, and discussion with students and preceptors, four nursing issues or topics in specialized areas of nursing.
2. Experienced an orientation to the Senior Focus Program: its goals, objectives and logistics. (New Preceptors)
3. Participated in a discussion of "Self-Responsibility as a Holistic Nursing Concept." (All except new preceptors)
4. Completed a component of the course evaluation tool used to evaluate students in Senior Focus.

Teaching Methods: Group presentations, small and large group discussion and lecture with various visual aids.

*PROGRAM:*

1:00–3:00 P.M. – Objective one.
3:00–3:15 P.M. – Break.
3:15–4:00 P.M. – Objectives Two and Three.
4:00–4:45 P.M. – Objective Four.
4:45–5:00 P.M. – Wrap up. Turn in evaluation and posttest. Pick up your CE certificate.

You are deeply appreciated by instructors, students, the Department of Nursing and the University. We are all aware of your commitment to the education of our students and hope you can come and be a part of this learning and sharing experience.

You are also invited to be involved in the student/preceptor group presentation. The students will be contacting you and getting your ideas. Each of the various areas of nursing represented will have about twenty (20) minutes to present something of relevance from that area to the whole group.

See you May 5!

*Source:* Senior Clinical Focus Faculty. Fresno, Calif.: California State University, Department of Nursing.

6. Prepare the documents required by the state for provision of continuing education units for nursing. The following are the requirements of the State of California; the requirements may be different in other states.

- Construct a posttest for the evaluation of the individual learning of participants that reflects fulfillment of the identified objectives for the seminar. Successful completion of the posttest qualifies the participants for the appropriate number of continuing education units. A sample posttest is shown in Exhibit 22–2.

- Prepare a certificate of completion of continuing education that includes name, registered nurse license number, social security number, number of units completed, date, name of participant, and provider number for the department of nursing. The document must be signed by the director (department chairperson) and the seminar coordinator (faculty member). A sample certificate of completion is shown in Exhibit 22–3.

---

**Exhibit 22–2** Preceptor Seminar Posttest

CALIFORNIA STATE UNIVERSITY, FRESNO
Department of Nursing

NURSING 128B1 Senior Clinical Focus

POSTTEST—PRECEPTOR/STUDENT SEMINAR

(BOTH GROUPS)
1. What evidence of cooperation/collaboration/interdependence did you see in the student/preceptor presentations? How do you see students using self-responsibility in these cooperative efforts?

(ORIENTATION GROUP ONLY)
2. Give two circumstances in which instructor intervention might be necessary in the clinical setting.

(ORIENTATION GROUP ONLY)
3. Outline the basic responsibilities of a preceptor.

(SELF-RESPONSIBILITY GROUP ONLY)
4. Give one way the concept of self-responsibility applies to each of the following: (1) Student learning, (2) Client care, (3) Personal health (mind, body, spirit), (4) Teaching/precepting

(BOTH GROUPS)
5. Choose one item on the conceptual evaluation tool and give an example of meeting that objective at each level of performance.

*Source:* Senior Clinical Focus Faculty. Fresno, Calif.: California State University, Department of Nursing.

**Exhibit 22-3** Preceptor Seminar Certificate of Completion

CALIFORNIA STATE UNIVERSITY, FRESNO
Department of Nursing

M. Jacque Cramer

RN LICENSE NO. N 241577   SOCIAL SECURITY NO. 432-56-9833

HAS SUCCESSFULLY COMPLETED FOUR (4) CONTINUING EDUCATION CONTACT HOURS ON
May 5, 1982.

PRECEPTOR/STUDENT SEMINAR

*[signature]* RN, MS
SEMINAR COORDINATOR

*[signature]*
CHAIRPERSON, DEPARTMENT OF NURSING

THIS COURSE HAS BEEN APPROVED BY THE CALIFORNIA BOARD OF REGISTERED NURSING,
BRN PROVIDER NO. 00176.

THIS CERTIFICATE MUST BE RETAINED BY THE LICENSEE FOR A PERIOD OF FOUR (4)
YEARS AFTER THE COURSE CONCLUDES.

*Source:* Senior Clinical Focus Faculty. Fresno, Calif.: California State University, Department of Nursing.

- Develop an attendance form to provide identification of those granted continuing education units. This form must show the name of the nurse, the social security number, the registered nurse license number, and address.

7. Make a program for distribution on the day of the workshop. The program should include the title of the presentation, the names of the speakers, and the names of the group members and agencies represented. It is also very helpful to plan a time frame for each part of the program and appoint a timekeeper to ensure that each person gets an allotted time for presentation.

8. Develop an evaluation tool to structure feedback from participants in evaluating the program and planning for future seminars. An evaluation form for this purpose is shown in Exhibit 22–4.

## EVALUATION OF THE EXPERIENCE

The immediate feedback received will reflect a general feeling and response of the participants to the seminar. The feedback can be measured by (1) the quality and intensity of the interaction participation during the meeting, and (2) the responses on the evaluation tool. Did the comments and evaluation tool reflect feelings that the seminar was an interesting learning experience and that the objectives were met? If the feeling response is positive, the acquired learning is likely to be applied in the preceptorship experience. However, further evaluation is necessary to determine the extent of application of learning from the seminar.

Evaluation at the level of affecting performance of preceptoring is more difficult to evaluate. The desired response on this aspect might develop over a period of months and be very subtle in form. Positive indications might include more effective and efficient use of the course evaluation tool. Another indicator might be students' comments to the effect that the preceptors seem to understand the course objectives and underlying philosophy.

The instructor should examine personal growth in planning and facilitating learning experiences for various groups of people. Relevant questions might be, Am I growing in my ability to plan interesting learning experiences that will accomplish the identified goals? Am I becoming more confident and secure in my ability to work with various groups of people and in different settings? What are the implications for my learning in the critical incidents that occurred?

**Exhibit 22–4** Preceptor Seminar Evaluation Form

---

CALIFORNIA STATE UNIVERSITY, FRESNO
Department of Nursing

Evaluation Preceptor/Student Seminar
May 5, 1982

Please circle one of the following numbers for each item.

1. What is your overall evaluation of this program?
   1        2        3        4        5
   Poor              Fair              Excellent
2. How well did the program meet the objectives?
   1        2        3        4        5
   Not at all                         Completely
3. How well was the presentation organized?
   1        2        3        4        5
   Poor              Fair              Excellent
4. The level of material presented during the program was:
   1        2        3        4        5
   Too simple        Just right        Too advanced
5. To what extent did the workshop contribute toward a better understanding of your role in Senior Focus?
   1        2        3        4        5
   Not at all                         A great deal
6. What is your overall satisfaction with time allowed for discussion?
   1        2        3        4        5
   Inadequate                         Adequate
7. To what extent did the program meet your needs in your individual situation?
   1        2        3        4        5
   Not at all                         Completely
8. What subject areas or issues would you like to be discussed in the next preceptor seminar?

9. Any additional comments, problems, or suggestions?

*Source:* Senior Clinical Focus Faculty. Fresno, Calif.: California State University, Department of Nursing.

---

## CONCLUSION

Preceptor seminars are a tool that can be used to increase the efficiency and effectiveness of preceptors in nursing education. A preceptor seminar is successful when the coordinator (1) is skilled in group leadership, (2) is able to communicate effectively with the involved persons, and (3) is successful in facilitating cooperative efforts between nurses and nursing students who have different interests and values.

Preceptor seminars provide an opportunity for a spirit of unity to develop between nursing practice and nursing education. Specialized areas of nursing have the opportunity to see similarities and basic concepts that apply to all of nursing. That, perhaps, is the most rewarding aspect.

# Chapter 23

# The Need for Faculty-Preceptor Workshops

*Sylvia Novak*

From the moment the education of nursing students began moving away from the clinical area into the academic setting, the gap between faculty and clinicians also began to grow. Because the preceptorship program brings nursing service and education back together and places them in different roles, it creates a situation that can either pose potential problems, or one that can be nurtured into an exciting and positive experience for everyone involved.

There was a time when those who taught nursing to the students were also the clinical role models. Because of the division of education and service, separate fields of professionalism began to develop. Nursing educators' views of nursing evolved of necessity into a broader concept—one that encompassed research, preventive and primary care, and professional idealism.

Meanwhile, the nurses whose professional lives had centered in the provision of traditional patient care became frustrated with graduates who came to the health care agencies unprepared for independent practice. The reasons for this are well documented in the literature (and amply defended by the schools!). Ways of alleviating the problem are now being explored. Dual appointments and other ways of combining the forces and the resources of education and service have been tried and found to be successful. But in many areas of the country, the duality of viewpoints in nursing is still very much alive.

## PROBLEMS INHERENT IN PRECEPTORSHIP PROGRAMS

In planning a preceptorship program, one can reliably predict two problems that are inherent in the role changes experienced by the participants. One problem is the discomfort that the clinical practitioner feels in the role of teacher. True, nurses are expected to include teaching in their practice skills, but the usual "students" of nurses are their clients and patients. Nurses teach everything from diabetes control to diapering babies. Only the faculty—nurses who have taken nursing education courses—are supposed to teach other nurses! Oh, yes, there are the inservice instructors, but that's different. Inservice instructors do not engage in everyday, one-to-one situations with inquisitive nursing students. The things students learn now-a-days! It is so embarrassing to have a student carry on about some theoretical notion that the nurse has never learned. And then there are the times when students ask *why*, and the nurse has forgotten! Clearly, preceptors can be very uncomfortable in the teaching role.

A second problem common to preceptorship programs is the concern felt by faculty about the loss of their control over a clinical experience, one that seems "out of their hands." Faculty have worked hard at developing objectives and content to meet the educational goals of the school. Will the preceptors be sensitive to these goals? Will they want to meet the identified learning needs of the students? Or will they ignore all that and do their own thing, and in so doing, redesign the course content? Perhaps the preceptor's philosophy of nursing is not in agreement with that of the school. Will some "bungling" preceptor undo everything the school has tried to build? The "reality shock" brought on by such a preceptor might scare the student right out of nursing forever! And let us not forget board approval or NLN accreditation. How does the school meet criteria set by these approval bodies for educational preparation of faculty through the use of clinical preceptors who often do not meet those criteria?

One solution designed to alleviate both of these problems is to have a preceptor-faculty workshop. Bringing faculty members and clinical practitioners together serves several purposes and offers a variety of benefits. The workshop is planned and organized by the school. One major purpose is to familiarize preceptors with key concepts of the nursing curriculum in general and the clinical course in particular. Not only should preceptors see how they fit into the course they are helping to teach, but they should also see how this course fits into the total program of the school. Knowing a little bit about the philosophy and objectives of the nursing program and the descriptions of the courses taken by the students helps preceptors get a "handle" on what kinds of information and experiences have been offered to the students. This presentation of content to the preceptors should be interesting and informative, but it should be reinforced by giving them written material to review and absorb later. Time is usually important and can be better spent in more participative activities. An example of a preceptor workshop format is presented in Exhibit 23–1. Examples of specific objectives of a preceptor workshop are shown in Exhibit 23–2.

**Exhibit 23–1** A Preceptor Workshop Format

---

*NURSING FACULTY AND AGENCY PRECEPTOR RELATIONSHIPS*
This one and a half day workshop will present the opportunities and materials for participants to meet the following course goals:

1. To provide a setting in which faculty and preceptors can meet and work toward shared or mutual goals in nursing and nursing education.
2. To identify ways in which a preceptor can become more effective in working with the student.
3. To identify methods by which faculty can improve their working relationship with preceptors.
   (Specific objectives are listed separately.)

The workshop is scheduled around the following format:
8:00 a.m. — Welcome and Introductions
8:30 a.m. — Videotape (Course-descriptive orientation, if available)
9:00 a.m. — Presentation "How to be an Effective Preceptor"
10:00 a.m. — Break
10:30 a.m. — #1 Work Group — "On Precepting" (See attached Learning Tasks for Work Groups)
12:00 p.m. — Lunch
1:00 p.m. — Feedback from Work Group #1
2:00 p.m. — Presentation "How to Work Best With the Preceptor Model Approach"
3:00 p.m. — Break
3:30 p.m. — #2 Work Group — "Faculty Preceptor Interrelationships" (See attached Learning Tasks for Work Groups)
4:30 p.m. — Feedback from Work Group #2
5:00 p.m. — Closure for Day 1

Second Day:
8:00 a.m. — Panel Discussion — "The Benefits and Deficits of Being a Preceptor"
9:00 a.m. — Brainstorming Session — Possible Topics:
          a) Should Preceptors Get C.E. Credit For Precepting?
          b) Should Preceptors Evaluate Students?
10:30 a.m. — Closure

*LOCATION*: The workshop for these two days will be held on campus. We have a very comfortable *lounge* area in the *University Center*.

*Source:* Rural Clinical Nurse Placement Center. Chico, Calif: California State University.

---

## PURPOSES OF PRECEPTOR WORKSHOPS

An understanding of the preceptorship program itself is critical. Here the faculty presenter can focus on the course objectives. This provides an opportunity to review the structure of behavioral objectives and evaluation of student performance. Many preceptors have not had an opportunity to acquire information or skills through the use of behavioral objectives. They need a thorough understanding of how the objectives are developed, guide

**Exhibit 23–2** Preceptor Workshop Objectives

1. The participants will identify through discussion and writing, how a preceptor functions as a *role model* to the student nurse.
2. The participants will identify through discussion and writing how a preceptor functions as a *resource person* to the student nurse.
3. The participants will identify through discussion and writing how a preceptor can better plan with the student in *designing the experiences* the student needs in order to meet his/her academic objectives.
4. The participants will identify through discussion and writing how a preceptor functions as a *supervisor* that provides the best situation for a student to become more skillful and able to identify areas for self improvement.
5. The participants will be able to identify at least two communication techniques to use between a preceptor and a student nurse.
6. The participants will be able to identify at least three common features specific to behavioral objectives.
7. The preceptor participants will be able to identify at least two behaviors they can observe for when assessing the student nurse.
8. As a result of listening and participating in panel discussion, the preceptors and faculty participants will be able to list the benefits and deficits of being a preceptor.
9. The participants will list at least two behaviors that: a) a faculty person, b) a preceptor can practice, that will stimulate change in the student nurse.
10. The participants will be able to identify two ways in which the communication and rapport between faculty and preceptor can be improved.
11. The participants will be able to identify resources and references that both faculty and preceptors can rely on to ensure the student's learning objectives being met.
12. The participants will be able to identify at least four behaviors from faculty that will assist the preceptor in working with the student nurse.
13. The participants will discuss at least three difficulties nursing faculty are confronted with in teaching nursing in order to help preceptors to better understand the academic environment.
14. The participants will be able to identify through discussion and writing what is meant by the term "learning experience."
15. The participants will identify at least two ways in which faculty can gain insight about the area/locale in which the student is being placed.

*Source:* Rural Clinical Nurse Placement Center. Chico, Calif.: California State University.

the student's learning experiences, and become the evaluation criteria in measuring levels of performance.

It is appropriate that the workshop leaders review levels of learning so that the preceptors can appreciate the careful choice of active verbs used in the objective written for each level, such as merely *naming* a group of items versus having to *compare* and *contrast* them. Reviewing this kind of information helps the preceptors see what is to be learned and provides guidelines for designing appropriate learning experiences.

Often new preceptors come to a workshop looking for specific answers to the question, What do I do as a preceptor? They have vague images of assigning tasks to their students and having them perform the tasks under their watchful eye, or maybe giving them separate tasks that do not require supervision but certainly help get the work done (perhaps they learned nursing in that fashion themselves).

A point can be made here: nurses who experienced all or part of their education in the academic setting rather than in an apprenticeship system are more likely to be comfortable with the teaching methods preferred by the school. The ability to identify more easily with the educational systems is the reason for the school's and the accrediting body's preference for BSN nurses to serve as preceptors. However, in rural areas this level of education in staff nurses is not often found—hence the importance of planning a thorough orientation to the program for the preceptors.

The workshop can serve as the beginning orientation program; but, in some cases, small group or individual orientation takes place prior to course commencement. Should the latter be the case, the workshop can be scheduled sometime during the course period, and it will function more as a tool for enhancement and follow-up of material presented earlier. Regardless of what purposes the workshop serves, the question, "what do I do?" should be addressed. Four main roles of the preceptor have been identified and exemplified in *A Role Guide and Resource Book for Clinical Preceptors* (Simon, 1976). Creative faculty could act out skits that demonstrate these roles and enable the preceptors to see themselves in similar situations. It is important to provide specific descriptions of the various aspects of the preceptor's role so that preceptors leave the workshop with a clear understanding of just what it is they do.

Principles of teaching and learning should be presented to meet the goal of assisting preceptors to be effective teachers. Active involvement in the learning process has been identified as a major enhancement to an adult's degree of absorption of content. Therefore, the information about effective teaching methods and factors in learning should be offered through small group activities. Some learning tasks for small preceptor work groups are presented in Exhibit 23–3.

Miniteaching projects can illustrate different teaching styles. Role playing and critique sessions can quickly identify the good and bad aspects of mock student-preceptor interactions. Use of videotape can be very effective if it is managed in a nonthreatening way. Most preceptors have never seen themselves on television. Exercises such as "Draw the Elephant," as illustrated in Figure 23–1, can help to demonstrate anxiety producing or reducing techniques in teaching.

**Exhibit 23-3** Learning Tasks for Preceptor Work Groups

*Work Group I* "On Precepting"
Choose involvement in one of the three following tasks:
  (1) Given an abstract goal, develop specific behavioral objectives to meet the goal.
      The Goal: "The student will gain knowledge and understanding of the role of the
          FNP (or PHN) in the health clinic."
      Desired Members: Faculty—1 or 2
                       Health Clinic Preceptors— 4 or 5
  (2) Given an abstract goal, develop specific behavioral objectives to meet the goal.
      The Goal: "The student will gain knowledge and understanding of the role of the
          acute hospital nurse in the clinical setting."
      Desired Members: Faculty—1 or 2
                       Acute Hospital Preceptors—4 or 5
  (3) Given a set of specific objectives, plan activities designed to meet them, and to
      function as criteria for accurate evaluation.
      Desired Members: Preceptors—5 to 7

*Work Group II* "Faculty/Preceptor Interrelationships"
Choose involvement in one of the four following tasks:
  (1) Develop a set of expectations; preceptor of faculty, and faculty of preceptor.
      Desired Members: Mixed Faculty/Preceptors
  (2) Given a sample evaluation form, design one applicable to nursing *students*. Consider: Health Clinic, Acute Hospital and Community Mental Health.
      Desired Members: Faculty
  (3) Given a sample evaluation form, design one applicable to *preceptors*.
      Desired Members: Preceptors
  (4) Optional Task: Given Carl Rogers' statement on independent learning, develop a
      mini philosophy of the preceptor's role.

*Source:* Rural Clinical Nurse Placement Center. Chico, Calif.: California State University.

In spite of the emphasis given to it in the preparation of the preceptors by the faculty, another learning experience should definitely be included in the workshop program: The preceptors should be given the opportunity to share with faculty their perceptions and feelings about nursing—extending from trends in general to particular role tasks. What do they think of the nursing issues currently being debated? Faculty may want to consider polling the preceptors prior to the workshop to determine what topics they would most like to have presented to them by a faculty speaker. These presentations could be designed to bring about discussion and encourage a sharing of ideas. Of course such presentations would have a lower priority and would be inappropriate for a short workshop, but they would fit nicely into a two-day schedule. The preceptors should be asked to describe what it is like where they are working. What are their needs? What satisfactions and frustrations do they experience? An excellent way to elicit this infor-

**Figure 23–1** Draw the Elephant

Group Exercise

The leader announces that directions will be given only once. No goal is indicated, and the directions are given quickly. The leader then proceeds to give verbal instructions on how to draw a certain figure, like the elephant shown below.

The exercise is then repeated (or discussed), utilizing goals (We are going to draw an elephant) and anxiety-reducing techniques, such as going slowly and offering repeated and explanatory instructions.

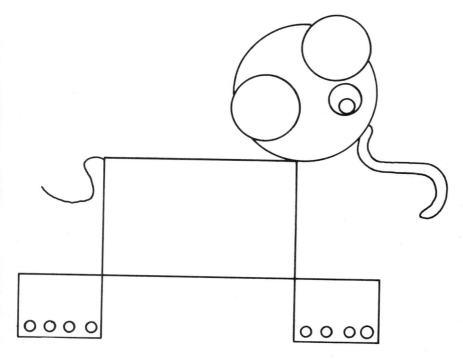

*Source:* Rural Clinical Nurse Placement Center. Chico, Calif.: California State University.

mation is to form small mixed groups of faculty and preceptors and give them the questions to discuss. Faculty could also ask the preceptors what their expectations are of faculty, and preceptors could ask for the same information from the faculty. An excellent way to validate accuracy in communication is to have a preceptor spokesperson from each group summarize what the faculty members said, and vice versa. This technique ensures careful listening by both groups. The summary speakers can then share what they learned with the total group.

Examples of topics and questions that can be dealt with in preceptor workshop discussion groups are shown in Exhibit 23–4.

Faculty are at an advantage in the workshop in that they know each other and have already engaged in ongoing group processes that have

---

**Exhibit 23–4** Questions and Topics for Preceptor Group Discussions

*General*:
1. Define cognitive and affective development in the learning process.
2. Identify how you as a preceptor can guide a student clinically in: a) cognitive development b) affective development.
3. What are some activities you can do with the SN that could be catalysts to that student's learning within a clinical setting?
4. What are some behaviors on a preceptor's part that lend toward poor growth and negative learning for a student in a clinical setting?
5. Define teaching:
6. Define learning:
7. Identify your role as a preceptor relative to: a) teaching b) learning.
8. Did you enjoy your clinical activities as a student?
9. Do you have a positive attitude toward education and teaching?
10. Who was your best clinical instructor and why does he/she rate high in your educational background?

*Preceptors*:
Please list what you expect the faculty person to do for you.
1.                              3.
2.                              4.
Please list what you expect to provide to your student.
1.                              3.
2.                              4.
Please list what you conceptualize that you are able to provide to the faculty person.
1.                              3.
2.                              4.

*Faculty*:
Please list what your expectations are of a preceptor.
1.                              3.
2.                              4.
Please list what you expect to provide your student through use of a preceptor.
1.                              3.
2.                              4.
Please list what you vision that you will be providing to the preceptors you utilize.
1.                              3.
2.                              4.

*Source:* Rural Clinical Nurse Placement Center. Chico, Calif.: California State University.

identified their common needs and concerns. Preceptors, in contrast, often do not know each other. In the workshop, not only are aspects that are common to most preceptors identified for faculty to absorb, but the preceptors themselves become aware that their concerns and feelings are often quite similar. This commonality of an otherwise barely acquainted group is supportive and reassuring to the preceptors. It is likely that, after getting to know each other at a workshop, some preceptors may make plans to communicate with each other to solve problems and share experiences.

## WORKSHOP LOGISTICS

Because preceptors are usually located in agencies throughout a large area, the choice of a site for the workshop should be made on the basis of several factors. If the school is not in the center of the area, an alternate central facility should be considered, especially if it is one that offers a scenic, cultural, or other added attraction. Timing is also important. Perhaps the preceptors can arrange for a weekend workshop that would not interfere with their work schedule. If the workshop is held on campus, faculty might offer a tour of the school to the preceptors. It would be particularly fortuitous if an on-campus event of interest were taking place at the same time and tickets were provided. Finally, it would be very helpful to budget for travel and lodging expenses for the preceptors, even if only partial reimbursement can be extended.

Incentives to encourage attendance by the preceptors should also be included in the planning. The opportunity for the participants to earn continuing education units not only makes the workshop more attractive but establishes it as a tax deductible educational expense. If possible, plan to provide texts, current articles, or other materials that the preceptors would find helpful and could take to their facilities. "Adjunct" faculty privileges, such as library and media use, are other attractive incentives to attend the workshop.

After the workshop, the faculty and preceptors willl be more comfortable in communicating and will relate to each other more effectively. When a faculty member makes a site visit to the student and preceptor, a rapport will already have been established, making the visit potentially more successful. The preceptor and faculty advisor are already beyond the initial phase of establishing a relationship. Seeing them work well together in pleasant harmony is supportive and encouraging to the student, and the positive role behaviors that are displayed will foster confidence in the student about nursing in general.

## CONCLUSION

The main purpose of a workshop is to help the clinical preceptor to become an effective teacher. This can be accomplished through orientation to the curriculum, presentation of information about teaching and learning, group discussion, problem sharing, and participation in role-playing activities.

A second purpose is to enable the faculty to learn about the clinical "real world" of the preceptors and to more clearly understand the preceptor role. Preceptors will gain satisfaction from the opportunity to tell the faculty what they expect or want from nursing education.

Several other benefits are realized by the workshop participants. Among them is empathy for others' roles and a greater acceptance of their separate, sometimes conflicting, values, needs, and styles of practice. Closer relationships develop between agencies. The workshop may instigate future collaborative efforts among them. Lastly, an important benefit that is difficult to identify but ultimately valued is the fact that the students are more likely to meet the objectives of their preceptorship course and experience greater satisfaction and higher learning in programs that have minimized their communication gaps and thus ensured their success.

**REFERENCE**

Simon, M.P.A. *A role guide and resource book for clinical preceptors* (U.S. DHEW Publication Number [HRA] #77–14). Washington, D.C.: U.S. Government Printing Office, 1976.

# Chapter 24

# Change and Innovation in Nursing Education

*Sandra DeBella Baldigo*

Innovation may well be considered a hallmark of nursing education and practice, as evidenced in the quality and quantity of the new ideas and approaches being presented in the many and varied nursing journals. Few other disciplines have changed so continuously throughout their history in education and practice.

The history of modern nursing can be viewed as a study in change. Indeed, one can say that change has been the one constant in nursing over the past decades, in fact over the past century. And there is no foreseeable end to the dedication to change and innovation.

## THE EVIDENCE OF CHANGE

One example of nursing's present commitment to new ways of doing things can be seen in the widespread use of technical innovations in nursing education, for example, the extensive use of computer-assisted learning devices and self-paced learning laboratories. Another is the establishment of new teaching and learning situations, such as preceptorship study. Preceptorship is a new idea based on an understanding of nursing practice that acknowledges the expertise of selected clinical practitioners while allowing them to share their knowledge with students who have selected their clinical areas for further study.

Nursing educators are also involved in the development of theory and research to support nursing practice. Nursing educators show a remarkable adaptability and flexibility in providing new settings for nursing care. They are active in all types of situations: acute hospital settings, public health department services, ambulatory care settings, senior centers, day care centers, patient care groups, self-help groups, and a myriad of other clinical environments. Nursing educators should be acknowledged and commended

211

for their energies, efforts, and continued creativity in support of nursing practice.

## THE ROOTS OF INNOVATION

A brief recapitulation of the cavalcade of change in the history of nursing would begin with Florence Nightingale, who emphasized that attention to the total environment of the patient—hygiene, nutrition, heat, and light—is as important as adherence to a medical treatment regime. This emphasis on total care was predicated upon complete dedication and commitment, as well as upon certain basic knowledges and skills that could be taught.

From this foundation, nursing developed as an independent profession. Nursing skills were developed under contractual agreements between the nurses, who were essentially in private practice, and clients or clients' families. By the turn of the century the training of nurses was moving into hospitals, which were becoming the primary institution for the care of the sick.

Nursing in the early part of the 20th century had three major foci, each of which was exemplified by an outstanding nurse: in private practice, Margaret Sanger; in public health, Lillian Ward; and in hospital nursing, Lavinia Dock. Ms. Sanger's experience in private duty nursing led her to the awareness that many women died from repeated unwanted pregnancies. She became the strong advocate of family planning and birth control, and she established her own birth control clinics. From her Henry Street House in New York City, Ms. Ward demonstrated the tremendous value of the school nurse in reducing student absenteeism due to health problems. She provided the impetus for the New York City Schools System to employ school nurses. In 1912, Ms. Ward suggested the use of home visiting nurses for industrial insurance policy holders of the Metropolitan Life Insurance Company. Also in 1912, the United States Children's Bureau was created. This had been the dream and goal of Ms. Ward for a quarter of a century. According to Kalisch and Kalisch (1978), Ms. Dock, a noted reform nurse in hospital nursing, stated, "I think nurses should stand together solidly and resist the dictation of the medical profession. . . . Many M.D.'s have a purely commercial spirit towards nurses and would readily overwork them" (pp. 285–286). This is a most timely and cogent observation that is still relevant in addressing a problem in nursing!

Licensing for nurses was established by the 1920s and 1930s, with some standardization of nursing education in hospital schools of nursing. Baccalaureate education for nursing was also initiated at this time. These five-year nursing programs had as their purpose and goal to educate nursing leaders in nursing education and administration. Through the 1940s, 1950s, and 1960s, the increasing complexity of patient care, the rapid development of medical technology, and concurrently increasing nursing responsibilities pointed to the need to include the basic preparation for professional nursing in institutions of higher learning.

In the 1970s and 1980s, nursing has been grappling with problems presented by the increased complexity of patient care in a vast array of new settings, by technological advancement, and by escalating nursing responsibilities in all areas of health care delivery. Nursing has developed expanded roles, clinical specialization, certification in the practice setting, and private practice. At the same time, nursing education struggles with the level of educational preparation needed for entrance into practice, that is, two, three, or four years of nursing education. It also struggles with the need for higher education for clinical specialization and for graduate education to develop nurse researchers.

Even in this cursory overview of the history of modern nursing, it can be seen that change has been a continuous characteristic of the profession. An analysis of modern nursing shows that its development and practice have been strongly influenced by its social context. It has been both influenced and informed by the "social revolution" of the past decades—by the wars, the public protest against wars, women's suffrage, civil rights, and social reform legislation that produced programs like Medicaid and Medicare.

## THE QUALITY OF CHANGE

But what of the quality of all these changes? Have they advanced nursing? Have they directed nursing toward the provision of better nursing care to patients and clients? What has been the rationale for change? Is this rationale in agreement with the essence of nursing practice and nursing development?

At this juncture, there is a great need to evaluate critically the rationale for change in nursing education and practice. We do not suggest that nursing halt or resist its pattern of change and innovation. Rather we submit that there is a great need for critical evaluation of planned changes in nursing education and practice. Our axiom should be: Beware of old ideas giving rise to change, when what is needed is new ideas resulting from new thinking and new attitudes that will support significant change and innovation. Change guided by old ideas results in rearranging the pieces of the orchestra while the same music keeps playing. It is cosmetic change only. It deals with the symptoms of the problem on an issue basis rather than with the issue as a whole. In contrast, rethinking some of the basic assumptions may lead to fundamentally new approaches.

The energy and the risks involved in making changes are an inherent part of nursing education. Nothing in a nursing curriculum is as constant as change. But the challenge is not to engage in change just for the sake of change, or because of external pressures. Rather change should be motivated and directed by a critical evaluation and analysis of the nursing process as congruent with the development of nursing as a practice profession.

A valuable experience in change can result from the self-evaluation of students, faculty, administration, and agencies involved in a nursing education program. How many times have we accepted as "inevitable" or as a "necessary evil" the level of frustration or anxiety experienced by students or faculty in meeting the demands and responsibilities of the teaching-learning situation? If education is to be a model for nursing practice, why should students, in learning about optimal health, wellness behaviors, and self-care concepts, have to experience excessive pressure or develop overwhelming (and unrealistic) expectations? The challenge is to create, in the most positive sense of the word, nursing curricula and learning experiences that model the wellness concepts we are teaching. Actions always speak louder than words.

## THE SONOMA SECOND-STEP PROGRAM—AN EXEMPLARY INNOVATIVE TOOL

The preceptorship course in the senior year of the Sonoma State University Second-Step (upper-two) baccalaureate nursing program is a prime example of innovation in nursing education. It is a learning experience that exemplifies change resulting from critical self-evaluation and provides an educational opportunity consistent with the learner's needs and with the goal of improved nursing practice.

The Sonoma Second-Step Program is founded upon the simple but radical idea that associate degree nursing education and its equivalent in diploma education programs can be considered the lower division nursing basis upon which upper division nursing can be built. The program includes many innovations that stem from this new concept. Community health nursing is the clinical focus of the first year. This provides the bridge experience for RNs, taking the students from the usual structured hospital setting and assisting them to use, develop, and enhance nursing skills, knowledge, and judgment. Community health also broadens the RN students' awareness of the context for health care delivery and of the complexities of the problems involved. The community health experience in the first year of the two-year program also bridges with the senior year preceptorship, which represents a positive, independent learning experience.

Preceptorship, as used at Sonoma State University, is a good example of new thinking bringing change that supports the essence of nursing. In the Sonoma context, preceptorship study is not an apprenticeship model of a master craftsperson teaching skills to a novice. It is rather the model of a practitioner with a certain level of skills seeking broader development through preceptor facilitation.

The preceptorship at Sonoma State University is described in the preceptorship handbook (Department of Nursing, 1976), which is used by faculty, students, and preceptors to direct the learning experience:

> The preceptorship in the senior year is a flexible approach to learning that allows the student an opportunity to explore in depth a chosen area of study and/or to develop expertise in a selected area of practice. This approach allows opportunity to practice self assessment, identify individual needs, develop behavioral objectives, select learning experiences, and work cooperatively and collaboratively with a preceptor, instructor and agencies in initiating the contract. Preceptorship study affords the opportunity to practice self-directed and responsible behavior, and practice as an active agent for change (p. 3).

The objectives of the two-semester preceptorship reflect the high degree of self-direction expected of the student. Upon completion of two semesters of preceptorship study, the student is able to:

- utilize problem solving and the nursing process in planning, implementing, and evaluating preceptorship study
- appraise the biological, psychological, and sociological characteristics of the client population for which the selected area of nursing practice is tailored
- formulate a knowledge base for the selected practice area from nursing and related sciences
- demonstrate skill in the techniques and procedures that are essential to the defined area of nursing practice
- demonstrate knowledge of the organization of the practice setting and its impact on the scope of nursing practice

- demonstrate interdependent, dependent, and independent nursing actions within the framework of the preceptorship (Department of Nursing, 1976, p. 8).

The self-directed nature of the Sonoma learning experience—with the faculty member and the preceptor serving as facilitators—creates an exciting, challenging learning opportunity in the practice setting. The reality context for the experience is excellent. Some students acquire a beginning level of expertise in a new clinical area; other students develop leadership abilities in selected areas of nursing practice.

The preceptorship at Sonoma State University is also undergoing change. A new dimension, an introduction to nursing theories, is being built into the preceptorship contract. The students in the first semester of the preceptorship will be exposed to a selected number of nursing theories. Then, in formulating the preceptorship learning contract for the second semester, the students will be required to include in the knowledge base a specific, self-selected nursing theory that they want to explore in the clinical setting. The inclusion of nursing theories in the knowledge base is seen as another step toward bringing nursing theory and nursing practice closer together. This goal is fostered by assisting the RN students to formulate their nursing practice based upon nursing theory.

## CONCLUSION

The advantages of preceptorship as a teaching strategy are of course not limited to RN students. A preceptorship is a valuable way to teach different types of nursing students in a variety of settings. Indeed, the gains from preceptorship study are not limited to the students. They also include benefits for the faculty, preceptors, and agencies involved in the coordinated self-directed learning.

In our personal experience as a faculty member who has served as a faculty advisor for more than 30 preceptorship students, we have learned a great deal from our students, and from their preceptors in their respective agencies. We have supported students who have ventured into new roles in nursing, such as nurse/ethicist, hospice nursing, and holistic health private practice. We have supported students who have taken leadership roles in more traditional settings, such as patient teaching, discharge planning, and cross-cultural nursing in ambulatory care settings. In each of these experiences, we have learned more about nursing as it is practiced in particular situations.

Preceptorship is an innovation in nursing education that has evolved in the history of nursing by building upon the firm foundation of nursing practice. It is an excellent example of change based on critical self-evaluation to further the development of nursing.

---

## REFERENCES

Department of Nursing. *Preceptorship handbook*. Rohnert Park, Calif.: Sonoma State University, 1976.

Kalisch, P.A., & Kalisch, B.J. *The advance of American nursing*. Boston: Little, Brown & Co., 1978.

# Bibliography

Baldwin, D.C., Jr. A model for recruitment and services—The University of Nevada's summer preceptorships in Indian communities. *Public Health Reports,* 1980, *95,* 19–22.

Bogner, H. How to keep the nurses you hire. *Nursing Life,* 1981, *1,* 18.

Chagares, R. The nurse internship question revisited. *Supervisor Nurse,* 1980, *11,* 22–24.

Chickerella, B.C., & Lutz, W.J. Professional nurturance: Preceptorships for undergraduate nursing students. *American Journal of Nursing,* 1981, *81(1),* 107–109.

Colon, K. Options for transition into practice: Nurse intern program. *Journal of the New York State Nurses' Association,* 1982, *13,* 7–10.

Dignan, M. et al. Internships and community health education: Is the juice worth the squeeze? *Health Education,* 1981, *12,* 42–43.

Everson, S. et al. Precepting as an entry method for newly hired staff. *Journal of Continuing Education in Nursing,* 1981, *12,* 22–26.

Friesen, L. et al. A clinical preceptor program: Strategy for new graduate orientation. *Journal of Nursing Administration,* 1980, *10,* 8–23.

Gibbons, L.K. et al. Nursing internships: A tri-state survey and model for evaluation. *Journal of Nursing Administration,* 1980, *10,* 31–36.

Knauss, P.J. Staff nurse preceptorship: An experiment for graduate nurse orientation. *Journal of Continuing Education in Nursing,* 1980, *11,* 44–46.

Kramer, M. *Reality shock: Why nurses leave nursing.* St. Louis: C.V. Mosby Co., 1974.

Lewinson, D. et al. Nursing internships: A comprehensive review of the literature. *Journal of Continuing Education in Nursing,* 1980, *11,* 32–38.

Limon, S. et al. Who precepts the preceptor? *Nursing and Health Care,* 1981, *2,* 433–436.

———— et al. The school-to-work transition in nursing: An annotated bibliography. New York: WLN Publications, 1981.

———— et al. Providing preceptors for nursing students: What questions should you ask? *Journal of Nursing Administration,* 1982, *12,* 16–19.

May, L. Clinical preceptors for new nurses. *American Journal of Nursing,* 1980, *80,* 1824–1826.

Mitchell, J.S. *Stopout! Working ways to learn.* Garrett Park, Md.: Garrett Park Press, 1978.

Murphy, J.L. Preparing a staff nurse for precepting. *Nurse Educator,* 1981, *6,* 17–20.

Nurse intern programs. *Nursing and Health Care,* 1981, *2,* 148–149.

Nurse intern programs. *Nursing and Health Care,* 1982, *3*, 164–165.

Nurse intern programs update—Institutions that sponsor nurse intern programs. *Nursing and Health Care,* 1982, *3*, 33.

Officers and Board of Directors of Nursing & Health Service. *Learning through experience in family health work.* Lancaster, Pa.: Science Press, 1944.

Olufson, E.M. An R.N. residency program in gerontological and long term care to improve job performance and job satisfaction. *American Health Care Association Journal,* 1982, *8*, 15–17.

Patton, D. et al. Implementation of the preceptor concepts: Adaptation to high stress climate. *Journal of Continuing Education in Nursing,* 1981, *12*, 27–31.

Plasse, J.J. et al. Preceptors: A resource for new nurses. *Supervisor Nurse,* 1981, *12*, 35–36.

Renetzky, A. & Kaplan, P.A. (Eds.). *First supplement to directory of internships, work experience programs, and on-the-job training opportunities.* Thousand Oaks, Calif.: Ready Reference Press, 1978.

_____ & Schlacter, G.A. (Eds.). *Directory of internships, work experience programs, and on-the-job training opportunities* (1st ed.). Thousand Oaks, Calif.: Ready Reference Press, 1976.

Rewards in nursing: Case in point "Nurse preceptors." *Massachusetts Nurse,* 1981, *50*, 6–7.

Roell, S.M. Nurse/Intern programs: How they're working—A survey of 43 institutions. *Journal of Nursing Administration,* 1981, *11*, 33–36.

_____ Nurse/Intern programs: How they're working. *Nurse Educator,* 1981, *6*, 29–31.

Searight, M.W. Preceptorship study: Contracting for learning. In M. W. Searight (Ed.), *The second step.* Philadelphia: F.A. Davis Co., 1979.

Simmons, P., & Haggerty, R. (Eds.). *The student guide to fellowships and internships*—By the students of Amherst College. New York: E.P. Dutton, 1980.

Stuart-Siddall, S. Backwoods nursing. *Nurse Educator,* 1981, *6*, 14–17.

Taylor, J. et al. Preceptorship is alive and well and working at the British Columbia Institute of Technology. *Canadian Nurse,* 1982, *78*, 19–22.

Treloar, D.M. Strategies for bridging the knowledge/practice gap. *Focus on AACN,* 1982, *9*, 12–14.

# Index

*Note:* Page numbers in *italic* indicate entry will be found in artwork.

# About the Editors

SANDRA STUART-SIDDALL, R.N., M.S., is currently the director of the Rural Clinical Nurse Placement Center, located in Chico, California. In addition to her teaching responsibilities, she is active in nursing politics and does per diem nursing in various health facilities. Ms. Stuart-Siddall has been a keynote speaker at many educational functions throughout the country. Her goals are to increase the number of nurses in rural areas and to promote the increased utilization of preceptorships in nursing education.

JEAN M. HABERLIN, R.N., B.S., received her baccalaureate degree in nursing in 1979. Since that time, she has been the clinical coordinator for the Rural Clinical Nurse Placement Center at California State University, Chico. She is presently pursuing a master's degree in business administration.

# About the Contributors

ANITA GORDEUK BACKENSTOSE, R.N., M.S., F.N.C., received her B.S.N. degree from the Pennsylvania School of Nursing, and her M.S. degree from the University of Utah. Currently she is an instructor of nursing at the Nell Hodgson School of Nursing in Atlanta, Georgia.

SANDRA DEBELLA BALDIGO, R.N., M.S., is an associate professor of nursing at Sonoma State University in Rohnert Park, California. She received her B.S. degree in nursing from the University of San Francisco in 1968, and her M.S. degree in community nursing from San Jose State University in 1973. Her professional experience includes 10 years' teaching experience and work in community health, as well as medical, surgical, and intensive care nursing.

BARBARA A. BERGERON, R.N., F.N.P., has been instrumental in establishing three new sites for clinics in remote areas of northern California. She is a graduate of the family nurse practitioner program of the University of California at Davis in 1976. Presently, Ms. Bergeron is employed by the National Health Service Corps at Butte Valley Rural Health Center in Dorris, California.

CLAUDE T. BERGERON, R.N., F.N.P., graduated in 1974 from the family nurse practitioner program, University of California at Davis. He has been active as a preceptor for rural clinical nurse placement students for the past six years and has worked at several remote rural sites in northern California. He currently serves with the National Health Service Corps at Butte Valley Rural Health Center in Dorris, California.

MONICA JEAN DAVIS, R.N., graduated from East Los Angeles College in 1976. She currently is working in the oncology ward at Saint Joseph's Hospital in Albuquerque, New Mexico. Ms. Davis also is attending the University of New Mexico to complete her B.S. degree.

LAURA DELUCA DOUVILLE, R.N., B.S., practices in the surgical intensive care unit at the Veterans Administration Medical Center in Cincinnati,

Ohio. She received her B.S. degree in nursing from California State University at Long Beach and, as a student, participated in a rural preceptorship program.

**ELAINE ELIZABETH DYE-WHITE**, R.N., M.S., Ed.D., received a bachelor's degree from California State University at Long Beach, her master's degree from the University of California at Los Angeles, and her doctorate from the University of Southern California. She is an associate professor in nursing at California State University at Long Beach.

**FRANK T. FARNKOPF**, R.N., P.H.N., B.A., B.S.N., graduated from the University of California at Berkeley in 1972 with a bachelor's degree in biological sciences. In 1978, he graduated from California State University, Long Beach, with a bachelor's degree in nursing. Presently he is director of nursing services at Seneca District Hospital in northeastern California. He also is an active member of the Northern Sierra Consortium for Health Sciences.

**ARLENE PARRISH GRAY**, R.N., M.S., is program director of a NIOSH-funded grant in occupational health nursing. Her professional experience includes acute care and community health nursing. She has taught community health nursing at California State University, Long Beach, and, for the past seven years, has taught community health nursing, nursing management and leadership, and occupational health nursing at California State University, Fullerton. Ms. Gray is working toward a Dr.P.H. degree at the University of California, Los Angeles.

**JANE HENNEMAN**, R.N., B.S.N., participated in the Rural Clinical Nurse Placement Center prior to her graduation from California State University at Long Beach. She began practicing at Seneca District Hospital in Chester, California, where she had been placed by the RCNPC. Ms. Henneman is the inservice coordinator at Seneca.

**KATHERINE JENSEN**, R.N., C.N.M., graduated in 1979 from Cuesta College in San Luis Obispo, California with an associate degree in nursing. She has recently completed the Nurse Midwifery Education Program at the University of California at San Francisco, and plans to return to rural community practice.

**JEANNIE B. MAES**, R.N., B.S.N., has been active as a preceptor for many years. She has also been involved in a northern California inservice education research project. Her professional experience includes psychiatric, medical, and coronary care nursing and work in community health. She currently is a nurse consultant with the Far Northern Regional Center of Continuing Care Services for the Developmentally Disabled, located in Chico, California.

**VIRGINIA YOUNG MEYER**, R.N., M.S., M.P.H., is a doctoral student at the University of California, Berkeley. Her professional experience includes public health and school nursing. Ms. Meyer has taught school health nursing and community health at the University of California, San Francisco and has been a faculty member at Sonoma State University for seven years.

SYLVIA NOVAK, R.N., M.S.N., graduated from California State University at Los Angeles, with a bachelor's degree in nursing in 1967 and an M.S. degree in nursing in 1972. She served as assistant project director for the Rural Clinical Nurse Placement Center at California State University, Chico, where she now is an assistant professor of nursing.

DIANE ROWE, R.N., M.S., is a graduate of the University of California at San Francisco's School of Nursing. She served as coordinator of the senior focus nursing course at California State University at Fresno, where she has been a lecturer for the past seven years. Ms. Rowe also does staff relief work with an emphasis in critical care nursing.

PHYLLIS SCHUBERT, R.N., M.S., is presently instructor/coordinator for senior students who have selected an area of focus in nursing and are placed in the community with preceptors. She is also completing course work for a license in marriage, family, and child counseling. Her professional and academic work has been done primarily in the areas of school nursing and community health.

SUE THOMAS, R.N., B.S.N., attended Loma Linda University, where she received her B.S.N. degree in 1979. During her studies, she participated in a preceptorship offered by the Rural Clinical Nurse Placement Center. She is now a staff nurse at the Indian Health Service Hospital in San Carlos, Arizona.

WENDY VOTROUBEK, R.N., B.S., is presently working for the Visiting Nurse Association of Los Angeles as a public health nurse. She is cofounder of DES Action, Los Angeles, and was a participant in the rural health option while enrolled for the bachelor's program at California State University, Long Beach.